Minimalist Budgeting

Grow Your Dough Budgeting Like a Pro

(How to Save Money, Spend Less and Live More With a Minimalist Lifestyle)

John Marks

Published By **Andrew Zen**

John Marks

Minimalist Budgeting: Grow Your Dough Budgeting Like a Pro (How to Save Money, Spend Less and Live More With a Minimalist Lifestyle)

ISBN   978-1-77485-926-1

No part of this guidebook shall be reproduced in any form without permission in writing from the publisher except in the case of brief quotations embodied in critical articles or reviews.

Legal & Disclaimer

The information contained in this ebook is not designed to replace or take the place of any form of medicine or professional medical advice. The information in this ebook has been provided for educational & entertainment purposes only.

The information contained in this book has been compiled from sources deemed reliable, and it is accurate to the best of the Author's knowledge; however, the Author cannot guarantee its accuracy and validity and cannot be held liable for any errors or omissions. Changes are periodically made to this book. You must consult your doctor or get professional medical advice before using any of the suggested remedies, techniques, or information in this book.

Upon using the information contained in this book, you agree to hold harmless the Author from and against any damages, costs, and expenses, including any legal fees potentially resulting from the application of any of the information provided by this guide. This disclaimer applies to any damages or injury caused by the use and application, whether directly or indirectly, of any advice or information presented, whether for breach of contract, tort, negligence, personal injury, criminal intent, or under any other cause of action.

You agree to accept all risks of using the information presented inside this book. You need to consult a professional medical practitioner in order to ensure you are both able and healthy enough to participate in this program.

TABLE OF CONTENTS

Chapter 1: The Minimalist Lifestyle

In this section, you'll discover the style of living that embraces minimalism as well as the various styles. Find out which one is suitable for you!

The Internet is filled with information and videos on minimalist living. A lot of people who live the minimalist lifestyle list 150 items they own, or 100 items they have. Some will live entirely in their own bag or even an empty backpack! It is not uncommon to meet the adventurous person who claims to have nothing but the shirt they wear! In the end, the person who has 100 things could tell the person with 150 items that they are not living a minimalist life. It's like an opportunity to determine who has the least amount of stuff.

However, the minimalist lifestyle shouldn't be reduced to the level of competition. You're choosing this way of life because you want to get the most of your the time you have. Be aware of that when you plan your life. Don't get swayed by the amount of stuff you own. Your lifestyle and dedication to minimalism cannot be measured by numbers! While reading this book, bear in mind that it is an actual guide, and not meant to be considered as an absolute rule. The minimalist lifestyle implies something distinct for every person and the activities and advice in the book are only that: suggestions. If something isn't to your taste, it's not essential to adhere to the advice, but bear on your toes that the primary motive behind this type of lifestyle is to live a life that is mindful and enjoy the best of life , while taking the least amount of effort. Remember this when you determine what is effective best for your needs and not.

Since the popularity of minimalism has increased, it has been a hot issue It has been met with some doubt. The most popular critiques is that minimalism only works to certain population groups. It is necessary to be single, have an income that is a specific amount, reach at a certain age and reside in an affluent nation.

Additional criticisms in the American context have suggested that it works only on whites. There's even a belief that minimalism is only for men , but not for women. I would like to challenge any of these myths. If you really desire to, then you should take a minimalist approach.

Be aware that not all aspects of minimalism will suit you. You aren't an exception to the rule even if you don't follow every element of the minimalist life style. Based on your personal circumstances you determine what you will accept as a minimalist. Keep in mind that you are able to try different things again later on and you don't need to test everything at once. The minimalists do not come from the ground They are created, slowly, but slowly! Living a minimalist life is to develop a desire to be more simple. Everyone could benefit from more appreciation and a sense of for the simplicity and happiness. This is achievable regardless of circumstance or the context.

If you are beginning your journey towards a minimalist way of life, here are a few points to remember:

* Don't think of yourself as a person who drink a lot simply because you've decided to reduce your consumption.

* Don't be a jerk when it takes you some time to implement any of the features of minimalist life outlined in this book. It isn't an endurance race!

Concentrate on minimal lifestyle prior to trying to lure people into your style of living.

* Minimalism is a method and not a doctrine with strict guidelines. It's not a requirement that you sell everything or do only the minimum. Living this way will teach you to make more measured choices as well as live life with more consciousness.

Be aware that your lifestyle could change and there could aspects of minimalist living that would be difficult to adhere to. There may be a outfit that you rarely wear now, however, if you get an executive position in an international company and you are expected to have a couple of suits. A minor change doesn't mean that you need to give up all minimalism completely. It is essential to consider what areas of your life are best served by the minimalist method - do not fret, you'll still be able to lead a in a minimalist manner!

The most important thing to consider it that this current style of living a minimalist lifestyle began as a reaction to the excessive consumption which is prevalent in our society. but it's not anti-shopping. If you do go on an occasional shopping spree at a time it is still possible to be a minimalist. The most important thing is to have things that have value and, if you buy more things, they must be useful or be of a long-term use.

Did I mention that you keep a notebook and pen at hand while you read this book? This is the perfect time to pull them out.

Look over the things you have and decide the things that are valuable and what doesn't. In the present it is not necessary to write everything down or be in the depths of your collection. This exercise can be a good prelude to living a minimalist life. Select a random number of 20-30 or even 50 items , and decide which ones hold a significant place in your life and are worth the cost. Did the guitar justify the cost? Yes! It's great for music and stimulates your brain. What's with your Santa Claus statuette that's in the attic, accumulating debris in an attic? It's only required to be removed at Christmas time or even after that it doesn't have to be removed. What happens to the lamp placed on the table by the bed? It surely serves a function. You could also switch on the entire light in your space and not use the lamp. Use the light source from your smartphone or small flashlight. Write down the things that you enjoy in your life and then a list of the things which do not.

Clean Up!

Then, move we're on to the next stage! Before you begin your spring cleaning, it is important to sort your belongings. Make a list of everything you have - absolutely everything you have! Here's how to break it into pieces:

* A list of DVDs, books video games, CDs, etc.

* Clothing articles

* Furniture: beds, desks, drawers, cupboards, chairs etc.

* Decor: curtains, antiques, set-pieces, paintings, sculptures, etc.

Of of course, your home will contain additional things like appliances, but they are the things that need to be regularly replaced. To live a minimalist life it is important to concentrate on things that last and be aware of which items can go and which you need to keep. Be aware that this isn't an issue of competition. Do not think that you must get rid of 50 things or 75 things, or even 100 items. Get rid of anything you consider to be unnecessary. It will be a struggle but don't worry. It is not necessary to be adopted overnight. it is best to make gradual changes!

Books

After you've put together a an inventory of your entire library it's time to cut out the ones that aren't needed. Here are some questions to consider:

* What's the time since I last read this book? Would I ever want to revisit it?

* Is this book outdated? Do you own an instruction book for Microsoft Word 1998? Don't throw it away!

Does anyone have digital copy or an Audiobook?

* Is this work in the public domain, and therefore easily accessible for free access through the Internet?

This book is accessible at all libraries? Are you able to find it to repurchase at all bookshops?

If the answer to one of the questions in the previous four are yes then it's time to either sell or give the book away or give to charity. You'll have noticed that there are questions about whether there's a digital version available for your book. Through the book, I'll talk about the benefits of moving to digital formats when it is appropriate. Although the process of digitizing all your material is not a requirement however, it is an option since it's a proven method of becoming minimalist. If you are planning to replace your DVDs, books and CDs using the digital format there will be less clutter within your physical space.

Wardrobe

Sometimes, a glance at your closet is the main reason for many people to opt for a minimalist life. Beyond your personal library Your closet is what is going to require cleaning most! Here's what to take into consideration before giving the clothes away or selling them:

* What clothes are essential to your daily life? Are you in a business setting and consequently require many suits? Do you

require a variety of uniforms? Do you require attire for colder climates?

* What clothes do not suit you? You'll be amazed at by how many of these items are hidden in your wardrobe!

Do you have clothes that are solely used use around the house? To sleep? To clean up messy days such as repainting the home?

* Of the course, you should not forget to put away your shoes!

If you're a corporate employee, it may be ideal to hang on to the various suits. If not, consider how you can reduce the number of suits to two and three suits. Do you own any items of clothing that fulfill an essential function that isn't frequently used? Perhaps you have clothes that are appropriate for outdoor activities however your life does not require a lot of outdoors work. Get rid of the majority of outdoor clothes. Are you living in the tropical climate? There is no need to dress in winter clothing to stay warm in Svalbard which is the northernmost city on Earth!

One trick to adopt an minimalist style of clothing is to use a predetermined number of hangers. If you own 40 hangers, then you should be able to only have 40 items of clothes. If you have clothing that exceeds the limit, get rid of some items. Another method is to put up a different item of clothing, rotate the hanger so that it faces you. Make this a habit for every piece of clothing that you hang. Once you've had enough, you can check to make sure that the hangers aren't facing you. They are the clothes you don't wear frequently. Check if they can be sold or given away.

Another principle you may want to adhere to may be to follow the "one in one out" rule. If you buy a new garment that is to be replaced by an item that you have already. If you purchase a brand-new set of pants, you should know the pair that you have and leave behind. Did you purchase an entirely new outfit? Now is the time to put down the old one!

In the case of shoes they must serve an important purpose or be removed from your closet. Shoes for formal occasions serve a purpose because they are required for formal events. There may be a need for one pair of shoes for running, a different pair to play golf as well as a pair for general sports. You don't require many pairs of these types of footwear. Two pairs of flip-flops to wear on the beach or for around the home will suffice.

Furniture and Decor

When it comes to furniture and decor it gets a little difficult. Before you start looking at furniture, take a look at the purpose the furniture fulfills. If you own an end table for your bed is everything you need placed on top? Do you have an built-in cabinet or drawers? They are filled with the most important things? What are the essentials? If they're almost empty, you could downgrade to a more compact bedside table, or eliminate the table in its entirety and locate a new home for the things.

What do you think of furniture or décor that doesn't serve an objective? Does your home resemble an art museum? Maybe those trinkets, paintings and sculptures ought to be removed. Do you have a lot of chairs, tables or cabinets? Perhaps it's the time to throw them away. One of the objectives of living a minimalist lifestyle is to ensure that all your possessions serve an objective or purpose. Apply that approach when letting go of the things you own and when making an investment.

A smart way to buy the latest furniture would be to pick something that is smaller and has less capacity. For instance, if you have a closet that has the space to hang clothes and some drawers, check whether most of the clothes are able to be hung up. Drawers should be used only for underwear and socks. If the clothes you have completely fit in the space for hanging, consider what else you can donate.

Similar to buying an end table that is full of drawers, you might be enticed to fill them up to the point of filling them to the top. If you have a smaller capacity, it'll make you think about and decide what can't be donated.

In addition to being a way of life one, you might have heard of minimalistism for its aesthetic. It is an artistic style which has been adapted into home design. It is not necessary to adhere to a certain style or design principle for organizing your personal or home space, but embracing a minimalist style will show you how to arrange your belongings to make it attractive and practical.

Get your notebook and pen and complete the following tasks:

* Do you have any areas in your home that you believe should be better organized? What would you like to make different about these areas?

* Is there an style you would like to emulate?

* How often do have to replace items due to chaos? Write down the top 10 things

that you're having difficulty finding : keys, wallets important documents, keys, etc.

Here are some suggestions that will enable you to make the most of your time when creating your home and organizing your home's contents:

Use a tray to store items on the go like cellphone, keys, wallet etc.

Make sure to keep your essentials within a specific area of your home, and If possible, close to either the entrance to your home or exit point from your home. The idea is that if you have to get the items you need, you do not have to scurry through the house to gather the items.

All clothing you wear should be stored in one spot Watches, accessories or jewelry should be stored in your closet with your clothes and shoes.

• Keep all things that are related in the same area For instance your DVD collection must not be far from the TV; all electronic gadgets, including batteries, chargers, wires cords and so on. should be stored in one spot.

* Arrange a specific space for a particular reason - for instance, should you wish to showcase all of your family photographs, you should find a space to store your framed photos as well as family albums, and so on. The photos are usually dispersed throughout the home however, for your own peace of mind, put them in one central place like the living room.

• Keep emergency and backup items stored in a central area such as first-aid kits as well as the iron and ironing board and tools. It should be simple to access and simple to reach in the event that there are children at home Adjust according to your circumstance.

* Try to store all silverware in one place in the kitchen rather than being spread out across different areas. The same goes for glasses, plates and coffee cups. Try to avoid reusing objects; you don't require multiple knives, for example. Store all storage containers in one central location

of the kitchen. Keep the condiments, spices, and powders, and other items in the same central space. Napkins, paper towels cloths, as well as all other cleaning items specifically for kitchen use should be stored in one location.

Here are some tips that you can use to organize and remodel your house, you'll discover the most efficient methods to maintain an organized home. The trouble of finding your possessions looking through your mess will disappear. I strongly recommend you do an Internet search to find out the ways that minimalists have organized their homes, as you will surely get ideas on how you can make your home more useful instead of treating your home as a place to store things!

Before we begin the next chapter, here's a bit of homework!

Note down everything you own , excluding appliances.

Find out if the item serves a purpose or function or function. You can either write a brief paragraph or two that highlights the significance of the item or use a checklist to mark "yes" when an object has a function or purpose and "no" in the event that it is not.

* Digitalize everything you can!

Redesign and rearrange at least one room of your home.

* Begin to give things for free; consider what you've not used for a while to decide what isn't necessary for your everyday life.

Chapter Summary

There are a variety of styles of minimalism. Find your own style and what doesn't.

It is important to give away your belongings is not as difficult as it appears You just need some strategy!

• Organize your personal space and determine the most important things you need to keep.

The next section you'll be taught the techniques of thriftiness.

Chapter 2: The Frugality

This chapter you'll discover the importance of frugality and why conserving money is among the main elements of living a minimalist lifestyle.

Frugality is a crucial aspect of living a minimalist life. Before diving into the details, be aware that frugality does not mean spending less or giving up what you would like to have. Frugality is designed to save you money, without needing to sacrifice the things you want to experience throughout your life.

Our society is a society that is characterized by instant satisfaction. This is what makes it difficult to live a minimalist life. The instant gratification of our lives leads us to consumerism which is the exact opposite of minimalist living. Since you spent your earnings instantly on a quick-fix pleasure and now you're stuck with long hours of working to save for that dream vacation. Therefore the first rule of financial prudence is to establish long-term goals.

Take your notebook and turn to a blank sheet and note what you think of the questions below:

How long do you have buying goals? Do you want to purchase an apartment? Perhaps a automobile?

• What's your current purchase objectives? Do you want to purchase an expensive new outfit? Do you have a DVD with a movie that you like? Restaurant dinner at a well-known restaurant?

After you've written these goals down, it is important to decide how your short-term goals can hinder or delay the achievement of your long-term goals.

If you want to go on three days of cruising in The Bahamas. The cost for this cruise will be $600 for each person. If you are traveling with your partner The cost for the cruise itself is $1200. Let's say it's the exact sum you earn over two weeks of work. In addition to the costs of beverages, food and on-board facilities, as well as purchasing items on island shops, you'll need to set aside the sum of $2000.

You may also want to treat your partner to a costly dinner at a restaurant that just opened. The restaurant is run by a celebrity chef which is why the prices can make your bank account shake. If you pay $200 for the restaurant, what do you have to pay? Most likely, you'll take part in the event and reduce your spending on souvenirs and gourmet dining. Are you required to buy new clothes? If the suit is priced at 600 dollars and you mix that with dinner at the restaurant you're left with $800. Now you have $1200, which is enough to go on the cruise however not enough to take advantage of the facilities on the ship and within The Bahamas.

It could take you about two weeks to recoup the amount you spent on your budget. This is the attitude that you should develop when it comes to financial prudence. Consider the advantages and disadvantages of your short-term goals , and examine how they might affect or delay those long-term plans.

A well-known expression that is often used to describe "collect the moments and not objects," which is a method to say that you should put value on the experience over material things. This is an essential aspect of getting the most of the smallest of things. In the last example on considering the long-term perspective the decision was to take vacation for a trip to The Bahamas over eating at the same restaurant and then buying an expensive new suit.

We are prone to place value on the material items above all other things however, we consider items that are valuable for a limited period of time. Do you cherish the present you received at Christmas? What do you think of your phone when it is updated? The money you spend should go towards things that cannot be accomplished in any moment however, they can create memories. It is possible to purchase a mobile at any moment or eat in an eatery at any time but probably, you can travel anytime.

Get your notebook ready and flip it to the blank page. Find the answers to these questions

* What are your most memorable five experiences you'd like to go through? A trip? Skydiving?

Five items you'd like to buy? Are they replacing an earlier model or are they an addition to the items you already own?

Based on what you've discovered, figure out the way a product will hinder or delay the chance to experience. For instance, if you purchase the latest version of a smartphone, does it delay your dream trip?

We'll revisit this exercise at the end of Chapter 3.

Debt

Being debt-free is essential. Sometimes the need for debt comes because of circumstances. However, you shouldn't be in debt because of spending money on expensive clothing, a perfectly cooked steak, or a brand new smartphone. The process of building credit is essential and crucial for many reasons, but it shouldn't be relied on to make every purchase. Make sure you pay off your debt in the earliest time possible and when you're able to complete the payment pay it in full!

Maybe there is someone you have known who uses credit every time they can but isn't concerned about their debts, and despite having the midst of debt, their spending habits aren't changing - thereby slowing the process of repaying their debt. It's often when people are being in financial trouble that they make the decision to adopt a minimalist approach to life. They choose to save money and sell their possessions with no prejudice in order to get rid of their debts as fast as they can.

While I'd like you to get the most of living life with minimal consumption however, you may have to forgo a variety of pleasures first in order to pay off your debts. It may be necessary to delay your cruise trip for The Bahamas or that dinner at the new eatery to get rid of your credit card debt. I guarantee you that once you're debt free you will appreciate it, and you'll be able to take the time and space to pursue your dreams.

It is important to note that this information is not financial advice. If you're struggling with debt, it's best to talk to an experienced financial professional. However, remember that the earlier you pay off your debt, the better! debt the better!

Digitizing

I've previously talked about digitizing. Although digitizing is not mandatory and could or might not be a good fit for you I suggest you take it into consideration as a means to live a minimalist lifestyle. If, as I mentioned earlier, you decide to digitize your media then your shelves won't overflow with books, DVDs or CDs.

Consider the other items you have that could be digitized. After you digitize your belongings however, you don't necessarily have to dispose of the objects; however, if you do need to, you'll have backup copies. It is important to note that certain documents, like medical records, tax records legal records and so on. might require a paper copy to be submitted, therefore avoid disposing of them even if they've been digitized.

Get your pen and notebook and try to answer the following questions:

* What important documents do you have that could be digitally digitized?

Do you have photos that you have printed that could be digitalized?

* What do you think of any letters that were sent by snail mail in the earlier days?

Based on the quantity of the printed and scanned documents you own, converting them could be a long process. However, do not fret that this process doesn't need to be done as quickly as you can. Spend the time to scan and digitize your documents and information. What isn't necessary to be stored as a hard copy may be put away. Digitalizing is a great method of removing unneeded clutter.

You Own Money, But Money Doesn't own you.

Don't believe anyone who claims contrary! There is a time in which we require money to satisfy our basic necessities. The minimalist lifestyle isn't trying to make you lose value for your money, but it's seeking to ensure that you are not restricted by your finances. In the same way that the minimalist lifestyle is not about possessions, but instead against being the owner of possessions, it is important to be sure that the accumulation, possessions or spending money will not the main the point of your existence.

Think about the way you've pursued money and how it affected your life. You may be amazed by the instances when you've put yourself in a financial bind that could have easily been avoided.

Get your notebook and pen and try to answer these questions in the greatest detail you can:

What is the frequency at which purchase items on impulse or without a reason? What is the total amount you spend?

* How many times have you been forced to cancel a social event or an important event in order to do extra work to make more cash?

Have you ever taken a day off and the day off you asked for?

Do you jump at the chance to substitute for a colleague and make more cash?

What are the most frequent times tried to get an increase in your salary due to the fact that you feel your current salary was not enough?

• How many times have you opted to work extra hours to earn cash to buy something you didn't have to purchase?

What are the most frequent times taken on an extra job or a one-time job to earn extra money?

* How long will it take to earn your pay?

* On an average how fast do you pay your bills?

* How many times have you earned extra cash simply because you're bored or felt there was nothing to do?

I know this is a lengthy list of questions, but it's exactly the way I'd like you to feel exhausted! If a lot, or even all these pertain to you, that means that you've exhausted yourself over and over again while trying to find money. This could be normal and essential due to your individual circumstances, but if you feel that the bulk of your money-related pursuit is due to any of the above mentioned reasons you might think it's time to take a more minimalist approach to money.

Shopping

In light of all this advice about frugality, it might be a bit odd to discuss the necessity of shopping. But , remember that shopping is a necessity , and the minimalist lifestyle isn't insisting that you do away with it. Brands with a name and luxury are not necessarily enemies of a minimalist lifestyle. It's just that minimalist living isn't a match for these brands as consumption is. If you are in the market for new laptops and you are not against minimalism, it's not a bad idea to choose the most current model from Apple or Microsoft and you don't need to get a $200 model that has limited capabilities. Choose a laptop that will meet your requirements and be trustworthy. It is a thing that you must cherish - just as minimalists ought to value all of their items. If you are planning to purchase an eyeglasses it's perfectly fine to buy the sunglasses from a reputable brand instead of buying an inexpensive pair at the neighborhood convenience shop. They should be valued as they shouldn't end up in an endless collection of glasses. If purchasing the most expensive glasses make you appreciate these glasses more, then it's absolutely fine.

Chapter Summary

*Frugality is the motto when it concerns minimalist living.

Be aware of the amount you are spending your money.

* If you are forced to shop, take measured choices about what you buy.

In the next chapter , you will learn how to organize your space to fit your minimalist style of living.

Chapter 3: Environment

This chapter you'll be taught how to create an environment that is conducive to minimalism. You will also learn how minimalism can be beneficial to the environmental!

Once you've removed your belongings and determined the worth of the items you've saved It is now time to get your stuff organized. For minimalists, arranging and arranging your space is essential. Look around at the various areas in your house. Are they better organized? As you become minimalist, these spaces need to be better organized!

The Office

If you go to your desk, or you are at it the majority of your working hours the desk needs to be properly organized. If your desk is equipped with drawers take them out and examine the contents. If your drawers are filled with things that aren't needed, look the items that can be put away or donated. The drawers should be stocked with only important items required for your work at your desk. The stationery you use should be abundant inside the drawers. If you keep a laptop computer at your desk, an extra mouse or charger could be stored in drawers.

On your desk Keep what you need to be utilized to complete your work. It could include your laptop computer as well as a legal pad. immediate stationery, such as sticky pads, pens and staplers. Additionally, you may need the lamp. Do not decorate you desk space with unnecessary decor like photos. These may appear to be something you would want to have on your workspace, but keep in mind that you're an affluent person! That's not to say that this stuff should be prohibited on your table, they ought to be only used in a limited manner. Desk accessories are there to serve a purpose or at a minimum can be of value. It is not a good idea to examine your desk and feel like it's overcrowded.

The Bathroom

The bathroom is often an area where clutter can accumulate. Take a look around your bathroom and consider what can be taken away. Here are some suggestions to create a minimalist bathroom

Make sure you have one toothbrush with you, one tube of toothpaste and one bottle mouthwash at a given time.

* If you frequently shave buy blades in large quantities. If not, you can keep a small box of blades. You could even consider switching towards an electronic blade. You'll find a wonderful method to reduce the cost of cutting blades and razors inside Chapter Four.

Take a look at the cosmetics you have within the restroom. If any of them is not being used on a daily basis, you can throw them out.

Limit the number of bathing and hand towels stored inside the bathroom. Make sure to keep one for each person in the household, but no more than two towels for each member.

Of course the bathroom does not have to be decorated or filled with excessive decorations.

The Bedroom

Bedrooms are typically multi-purpose. If you can divide bedrooms from work space it is recommended to achieve that. If not, be sure your work space isn't a burden on your bedroom. To have a minimalist space the bed should be the primary focus of the space. The bedroom should not contain any other clutter, If it can be facilitated.

Bedrooms are often stuffed with decorations, however, as minimalists one, it is best to just have decor that serves an important purpose or adds value to the overall look of the room. A painting that shows your personal style is a good idea as well as a few photos framed are also great options.

Clutter

At times, when moving into our new place when we move in, we gaze at the space that is empty and ask ourselves, what else can be done with it? We might even brag on how much we've planned for the material items that can fill this space. However, if you're an individualist - when you spot some space that is empty don't think about filling it with stuff without a reason. It's okay to locate an empty space in which you can put the spare bed, desk or even your luggage. There is no reason to fill it with things you don't need over time or on a regular routine.

The biggest obstacle to getting rid of clutter is the sentimental value that a tangible item could have. This is perhaps the reason we're hoarders! As I've discussed consumption, it has caused us to spend money on goods which provide us with some temporary pleasure. Certain items provide us with sentimental value as we experience a feeling lack of satisfaction in the absence of them.

Keep in mind that there is no obligation to sell anything, simply evaluate the value or purpose it plays in your life. There are a few things to think about when evaluating the sentimental items you have:

* Will this item add value to the life of someone else? Perhaps you appreciate the clothing of someone you love dearly. But, someone else might be in need of or greatly benefit from this piece of clothing.

* Is this item digitized? Like we said sentimental photos or letters can be digitalized. Things like diaries are also digitized.

* Is this piece an expense to keep? Maybe you own furniture or an old antique that is in the family for many years. But keeping it is more stressful than happiness. Think about selling it.

* Can this object be gifted to a loved one? You don't need to throw away a treasured possession maybe you could transfer it to a friend or family member.

In creating your surroundings You want to live your life with a sense of purpose. Your possessions or items that you purchase must serve a function in your life. When you are cleaning out the clutter in your home, consider what's unnecessary and should be donated. Another consideration is: do you have an easier alternative? Have you got a wall clock mounted on your wall? Since there is an endless variety of ways to monitor the time online is it really necessary to require a clock? This is especially used for furniture and decor. Be sure to remove objects that don't serve any purpose, or substitute them with a more practical alternative.

Have you ever lost anything in your childhood? I'm sure you've lost a toy , and it caused you to cry upon the loss. After a while you can move on and don't think about the toy. It is possible that you did not even know it at the time, but you realize that the toy isn't important and doesn't add value to your daily life. You probably also played hide-and seek and remembered the rules. Here is a brand new game that involves items and hidden objects:

* Pick an item that you're not sure about; you may think that it is of no value, yet you are hesitant to donate it.

* Displace the item. Naturally, you'll keep track of where it is but make sure to put it away in a location that isn't easily accessible. If, for instance, you're unsure whether you really need that $300 fountain pen put it in a secure place or placed on a high shelf anyplace that isn't accessible while you're working on your workstation.

* If, after a week, you're no longer enticed to purchase the item and you don't attempt to get it back then it's the time to say goodbye. of your ways.

If you've gone through this article, I'm sure you've shivered once or twice at the possibility about giving up your most prized items. Many people will promote the giving of things without considering. When you've hoarded things and have no idea what to do with them, they suggest you donate the bulk of your belongings in hoards! Although there's no problem with this strategy however, I will suggest taking a slow and steady route to getting rid of clutter.

Get your pen and notebook and write this down:

Note down the particular areas of your house that have the most clutter. For instance, you could say that your closet is overloaded with clothes. The table in your bed is full of clutter. The small cabinet in front of the door.

Have a quick look at these categories and select at least one item that you'd prefer to give away right away. You are able to choose any number you believe essential, but make sure you have at least one item.

Make a timeframe of not more than one week for the date you'll be giving the item away. For instance, "I will give away my brown dress shirt one day from now," and "I will give away my baseball bat in three days from today."

Be sure to follow all the way! If you plan to visit an auction, secondhand store, or a friend's house arrange a time in your day to hand out the item. If you choose to donate the baseball bat an area school to be used by the baseball squad, be sure that you make an appointment with the school the day you'd donate your baseball bat.

This is a good practice to begin with. In the end, it will help you develop an understanding of discipline and allow you to let go of things you no longer require.

Before we get started Here are a few quick techniques to speed up the decluttering process when it comes to stationery

* Take note of the amount of pencils and pens are available in the house, and dispose of any excess amount. It is your choice to determine what is excessive, however, five pencils per person in the household ought to suffice.

* If you own other writing tools like markers, you should only keep the ones that you typically use. If you use only black permanent markers, then the other colors must be disposed of from your house.

41

* You will only require one stapler, a couple of sharpeners, one hole puncher and one tape holder.

Zero Waste

This is one aspect of minimalism that is not often talked about, yet I am sure it to see it gain momentum quickly. The benefits of decluttering and making sure that clutter doesn't be able to enter your space again can lead to the goal of Zero Waste. Based on the location you live in and your life style, Zero Waste may not be possible, but you should consider what you can achieve. It's one of the most environmentally-conscious aspects of a minimalist lifestyle and can benefit both the environment and your own personal life - and your savings account.

Here are a few things to help you start:

Also, you should digitize all paperwork, and then dispose of it. Don't discard important documents, such as medical records or other legal files because a copies of them may be required in the future. Do your research regarding this issue.

* Make sure you have as few plastic bags around the house as is possible.

Find alternatives to buying water bottles made of plastic. You can also find alternatives to storage of these liquids at your home. If you are going to the coffee shop, ask whether they will serve your coffee from the thermal bottle you have. Some shops won't permit their staff to make this happen, but be patient but being environmentally friendly is becoming more popular and more and more establishments are likely to follow suit!

* Shop using your cloth bags. Check if your purchased items can be kept in the cloth bags you carry. Some shops won't permit this, so remember to be patient and patient with the store.

You should respectfully decline any free , non-disposable present you might get from a university campus, fair, festival or other event. It is one of the main factors that contribute to the mess within our homes.

* If you require information from an advertisement instead of getting print-ready copies of the flyer, you can take pictures of the flyer or record the information on your smartphone.

Make sure to send your documents digitally and avoid printing anything if you are able!

Travel

One of the most significant groups of minimalists are travelers. No matter if you're nomads or just travel at a time There is an approach to travel that is minimalist that can be extremely beneficial. Have you ever traveled to a new location and, from the appearance of your bags, it could seem as if you were moving to the area? The minimalist approach can teach you to be more compact and precise when packing, regardless of whether you're actually moving.

Here are some excellent ideas:

* Opt for smaller electronics. Try to carry an iPad instead of laptop. If you need a laptop look into whether it's possible to trade in the model you have currently in use for a lighter, smaller and smaller model.

* Roll your clothes instead of folding it; this will take up less space in your bag.

Try the minimalist wallet? We're told not to "fatten our wallets" however a simple wallet can carry all the essential licenses, cards and the amount of cash you require.

* For longer journeys it is possible to skip the toiletries and buy them when you reach the destination.

* Unless you truly require it, do not fall into the duty-free shops at the airport!

Chapter Summary

* You can create your own space to tie to your minimalist style.

* You can be especially aware and follow the Zero Waste lifestyle.

There are ways that you can make the most of minimalism when it comes to the travel arrangements you make.

In the next chapter, you'll discover how to be more mindful in the way you spend your money.

Chapter 4: The Deliberate Spending

Within this section, you'll discover how to manage your spending mindfully and consider your possessions as valuable.

We've talked a lot about the best ways to dispose of items you no longer require. But I've also stressed that minimalism doesn't mean buying things. The goal is not to deter shoppers from buying however to help you to be more careful with your buying routines.

Be aware of these aspects before you embark the next trip:

* Are you purchasing products that have a purpose? Are you buying a brand modern kettle? A coffee maker? A rice cooker? A portable GPS system to use traveling? New running footwear for your next race? A new laptop because the one you have is tired and worn out? Are you adding clothing to your wardrobe that you don't really have the need for? If you already own an amazing run-in shoes are you in need of anotherpair?

* Do you have plenty of room within your house? Have you ever bought groceries and had trouble putting them in the fridge? Your belongings ought to easily fitin the refrigerator; If they aren't, you might want to free up some space prior to buying something new.

* How long do you plan to maintain this present? Do you want to purchase an item for yourself as a present that will be thrown away or replaced at the next Christmas?

If you have ever made an inventory of the things you want to buy prior to making a purchase, you should take these factors into consideration. Your list of things to purchase is bound to be reduced as your purchases become more thoughtful.

The above approach is also effective in budgeting. The minimalist approach to budgeting can help you consider a variety of factors into consideration when deciding on how much of your budget needs to be allocated to various purchase. One of the things that the minimalist lifestyle and this book encourages is living your life to the fullest. I'd like to see minimalism enable you to live a more fulfilling life than what you're experiencing currently and the quality of your life will increase thanks to the minimalist lifestyle.

The primary aspect of improving the quality of life for people is having freedom. We often associate the size of our money with our freedom. However, if your money is constantly spent are we truly enjoying freedom? Being minimalists will require you to scrutinize each purchase , and take measured decisions about future purchases.

Unforgiven spending

Pause. Let me ask you to reflect on the time you bought something, but afterwards regretted it. You regret it because you realized that if you had stayed clear of this purchase, you would make a better choice or used the money to buy something else. Do you remember the instance of paying $200 for expensive food and the money could be put towards a trip in The Bahamas?

Take your pen and notebook and try to answer the following questions:

* What was the purchase that I made that I regret later?

* What made me regret it? Was it an unnecessary expense? Could I have got the best deal? Would the money have been better spent towards something more beneficial? Have I gotten into debt due to a frivolous purchase?

Write a few words in response to these two questions. After that, think about it for a while before continuing reading.

If you've been thinking about the purchase, I'm sure you're kicking yourself over a mistake you made. It will stop when you start making sensible choices. You may have heard about "If...then" phrases in computer science. I'm going have you use this method to make decisions when shopping.

Here's an example Imagine this: You're on your lunch break from work. After you finish your meal, you opt for dessert. It is not necessary to have dessert as your appetite has already been satisfied by the dinner. The dessert is priced at $8 and is a depreciating amount to you. Therefore, you aren't thinking too much about spending the money. It could be a small amount and you might not have the opportunity to buy something different. However, if you think you spend 8 dollars per day at work, and assuming it's five days a week, you will have invested $40 in the course of a week. It may seem like a lot of money. You might think like spending the $40 you're not giving up something. However, suddenly you discover that your favorite artist performs a show in your town and the price is $40. When tickets start being sold, you're in a an economic bind and cannot afford to pay $40. It's at this point that you realize that ordering desserts isn't enough to allow you to buying tickets to the concert. If you are spending $40 in a week on desserts, you'll be unable to attend the show.

This is only a minor instance, but the same mindset is a good idea to apply when making larger decisions. Imagine you're planning on buying a car. You have to make a $300 payment each month for a period of a couple of years. If you're unable to pay the minimum amount the interest is added to the $300. In the event that you are able you may be able to pay the minimum amount and make the payment earlier. If you set the decision to do this and sticking to it, you'll make sensible decisions regarding your purchases. You won't spend your money in reckless ways. Therefore, if you steer clear of buying things that aren't necessary and purchases, you'll be able to repay your car in time or sooner!

The minimalist method should teach you not to make purchase decisions on impulse and to make sensible decision-making in advance. You may recall that my post about evaluating your short-term purchasing goals and comparing them to your long-term goal for purchase. I would like you to go back to this exercise, but applying the "If...then" method to your objectives.

Take a notebook and pen, and make a list of three purchasing goals, and three long-term purchase goals. Examine how the short-term goals could influence those long-term objectives.

Here are a few examples:

* If I buy a new flat screen TV that is, it will take me another six months to repay my automobile.

* If I frequently have an espresso every morning before going to work, I'm spending about $25 per week. That's about $100 per month, which I could use towards booking a stay at a hotel in the next six months!

* If I put $1000 to purchasing Christmas presents then I might not be able to allocate $1000 for my tuition, which I'll be owed in three months.

Use this method to plan how you will manage your finances and purchasing. It is best to eventually adopt this mindset each when you purchase. This will help you to become a minimalist who can make prudent financial choices.

Food

Be assured that I'm not asking you take the diet! A lot of minimalists adhere to certain diets however, I'm not going to insist that you indulge in any way or follow a trendy diet, or eliminate every food item from your diet. There are many options available, and can bring a lot of simplicity to your lifestyle, however I'll look at how to manage your eating habits from a fiscal perspective.

In the same vein as spending $40 per week on desserts Take some time to consider the amount you pay for extra or excess food items. Don't include the food items you'll need to buy right now. I'll expand on this in the future. Start by focusing on the frequency you dine in restaurants and the amount you spend. It doesn't matter if you have already done it or not you should keep receipts for ordering take-out or food items and store them in a safe place for to use as a reference. It is essential to use these receipts during the next activities.

We will begin by the recording of eating out and restaurant expenses. Get your notebook and pen , and record these things:

Note down the amount you spent on restaurants or dining out during the preceding month. If you're able to do it more quickly I suggest you record as many months as you are able to return and determine the total as well as the average amount you that you have spent in the time frame you choose.

Take a look at the receipts thoroughly Note how often you purchased an appetizer or dessert for you. Estimate the total amount and also the amount you that you spent on desserts and appetizers. It is possible to separate these two categories or group them together.

Note down each time you ordered an alcohol drink that was not complimentary; in essence every time you didn't purchase water! Calculate the total cost and the amount you for these drinks. Do not record times you ordered a huge pitcher of beer to serve at the table. Focus on the drinks that were only meant for you.

Once you've got these figures in your account, I'd like you to consider where the money might be put to use. Let's suppose you spent 700 dollars at restaurants during the month. You also spent $300 on food, desserts and drinks. With that amount, you can make a monthly payment towards the purchase of a car, as in the example I provided before the outline. It could be used to fund other adventures during your next vacation. It could be used to purchase university textbooks or pay for an undergraduate course. It is also possible to save it and begin the routine of saving $300 per month, which is equivalent to saving $3600 each year.

Also, although I'm not saying you should not order desserts, appetizers, or drinks, the next when you dine out, consider whether you require these extras. If your main meal is enough to satisfy your cravings, do you see any need for appetizers or desserts? Make sure to drink the water whenever you can and eat Your financial account will be thankful in the future! Keep in mind the "If...then" method for any kind of purchase, such as ordering take-out or dining out are all things that should be dealt with using the most basic method.

We'll now move to the next part of spending money for fooditems: grocery shopping. Keep your receipts the time you buy groceries to keep on your journal.

Note in your journal: note the following information:

* The amount you spent on groceries over the course of a certain time frame - remember the longer the time more favorable.

* Describe how much money is spent on specific groups of items, such as what is the amount used on vegetables and fruits as well as meats, drinks snacks, desserts, etc. Reduced one-time purchases like when you spent a lot on birthday cake the month before. Make sure you are making regular purchases.

Note down the frequency with which these items are used: are your vegetables and fruits consumed frequently? Do you let your pasta stay on the counter for several months in the time it is cooked? Do you have soup cans that have expired date but you didn't even try to eat them?

Shopping for groceries is essential and you're likely overspending when you shop for groceries. Again, we'll employ a minimalist approach in order to cut down on our spending and thus improve our living quality.

Go to a blank page in your notebook. Write in the responses to these questions.

* Which things on your list of groceries are not essential? What items do you use only every once in a blue moon?

* What things on your list of grocery items don't seem to be consumed?

What items from your grocery list will take you the longest time to consume?

Maybe you purchase an ice cream tub and then use it as a treat every now and then. This is one example of an unimportant product. Perhaps you purchase soda or other drinks with high caffeine levels to prepare for a hectic day at work. Cut back or get rid of these drinks to save money.

What can't seem to be suitable for consumption? If it's the soup cans, then they must be taken off your list of shopping. If you find items that take a bit to consume, they should be taken off of your list.

Here's a challenge to do: during your next grocery trip Make sure to only purchase most essential items. Get rid of any unnecessary purchases. Examine the total cost of your bill to your previous bill, or with a bill with a lot of unnecessary things. Consider how much you saved , and then write down at least three items you could use the money to pay for. The possibilities are as easy as paying your bill faster or treating yourself to the movie or as a way to save towards the long-term goals. This analysis of your expenditures will reveal how reducing your spending will improve your enjoyment of life and provide greater rewards and reward.

Don't Forget This!

Discounts are a minimalist's greatest friend. As you've read, one of the main goals of a minimalist budget is saving money while spending less. There's no reason to not be spending money, and it is inevitable that the money must be spent. Therefore, why not make savings even if you have to spend it? Here are some ways to save money when shopping:

Make sure you look for coupons. Coupons can be found from a wide range of stores on the Internet and through apps and even inside your mailer.

* If you are able, hold off buying until sales are on. At certain times of the year or day, there could be significant discounts on products that otherwise wouldn't be available.

Check out different ways to purchase an item. It is possible to go into a bookstore and discover a book that you like for $20. On the Internet doing a quick search will reveal a variety of online stores that might sell the same book at an affordable price. If you're okay with purchasing a second-hand copy check out the internet for an alternative that is less expensive.

* Avoid spending a lot for one-time purchases when you can. Let's suppose you reside in a place that is warm all the time all the time. For winter, every holiday, you will visit family members who reside in a cooler climate that is snowy. In order to make this short trip you'll require a couple of winter clothes. After the trip, the clothes won't be worn for another

time until the next winter trip. It is not advisable to spend much on the clothes. Keep in mind that they're not commonly used, and if they do wear beyond them you'll be required to purchase them once more. Find the cheapest price you can without compromising in terms of quality. Also, if you reside in a cold climate , and you visit a beach on a tropical island every year, there's no need for you to buy a variety of swimming suits!

* Rent or borrow when you can. If you're going to one wedding per year and you are required to wear a formal or tuxedo dress What would you spend on the formal dress or tuxedo? It is more beneficial to borrow or lease the outfit for your wedding, and then return it later.

Earn rewards towards purchases. Maybe you have a credit card that offers points upon making purchases. These points can be used towards purchases in order to get discounts. Certain credit cards give points in the form cash. If so you could be able transfer the cash into an account at your banks!

* Another method of obtaining an offer that is also tied to financial sanity: if you get the gift card, make sure to use it! If possible, you should not purchase anything that is more expensive than the amount of the gift card, or make sure your card can be sufficient to cover more than half of the total cost of the products.

One thing to be aware of A minimalist is an experienced researcher. You should be relentless in your search for the top products at the lowest costs. Be aware that the cheapest price shouldn't be the same as the best quality. If the price is very high, but the item's quality must be equal. If you're purchasing something tangible, be sure that it lasts for an extended period of time. A single purchase of durable goods is more affordable than having to purchase the product at a lower cost frequently.

For instance, you can research alternative options for buying items at a lower cost.

I've given an instance of buying something in a bookshop instead of on the internet, but it does not end there. Similar to how I've advised you to be persistent in reviewing your purchases and pondering the advantages and disadvantages and the benefits, I want you to do your study. Always consider what alternatives are that are available. Here are a few examples that you might want to consider adopting as soon as possible:

* To shave razor blades: Razor blades are expensive. Check out subscription services for women and men which are cheaper and will send you razor blades monthly or as required.

* For clothes: There are a myriad of choices - there are always thrift stores and charity shops where you can purchase second-hand clothing. Shop at outlet stores to buy designer clothing at a discount. If you are able, limit your shopping during the seasons when sales are prevalent. There are many

subscriptions that provide you with brand new clothing from designers every month or on a regular basis.

* For transportation: If driving your car isn't required, consider alternatives like public transportation. If biking or walking are options, then consider these routes! As minimalists, your attention should be on safety as well as comfort and safety and not on the aesthetic appeal or the status that a car can give you.

* If you have the time do it yourself, go for it. Learn more about this in the following article:

Do You Do Your Own DIY?

We've become used to having the least complicated tasks carried out by others. If we don't have the enough time to tidy up the mess at home We hire an employee to take care of the house. You can also employ a cook, or go out to eat or request food items to be delivered. If the home requires maintenance, we have many people to contact. If we have to wash our cars, we look for an alternative or head to a car wash with a drive-through option and let the machines take care of the work! However, as an individual, you should take every chance to make it yourself.

The first step is to think about cleaning your vehicle. If you haven't done this now, consider the amount you pay each year to have your vehicle washed. Depending on how frequently you wash your car it can differ dramatically. But, make use of the concepts you've learned to determine the possibilities you can make with the money you've saved. I'm sure that regardless of the amount, there are more worthwhile things to do with the savings.

Cleaning your home is among the top priorities on any "most unpleasant task" list. One of the main reasons is being aware that cleaning the house is an extremely long and difficult task. Yet, many minimalists do not feel stressed when cleaning after clearing out. After you've decluttered your house, you can begin to clean it. You may be amazed to discover that you aren't finding it as difficult as prior to. In addition you'll save money and being more frugal, that's what minimalism is about!

There are other things that you could try to complete yourself. They may or might not be a good fit to your advantage, however consider what you can do:

Cut or style your hair yourself. Try to avoid an appointment with a barbershop or stylist.

• Repairing of appliances.

* Additional work is needed around the house , as in addition to home improvements and repairs.

Sewing is a great method to repair clothes or create your own!

Learn to become a computer specialist so that you don't have to take your laptop to the shop if the issue occurs; this expertise can be used to solve any hardware-related issue , such as fixing cracks in your screen on your smartphone.

• Learn skills like programming so that you can create an application that meets your needs and not have to buy the software you already have.

Learn a new skill that you contract out to someone else in relation to your professional. For example, if , for instance, you require a website to showcase your skills and resume, it's cost-effective and time-saving to create your own website rather than employ a professional web designer.

Learn to file your own tax returns. To ensure your security it is possible to use an expert, such as an accredited public accountant however, there's no harm in learning about the process yourself.

* Polish and fix your shoes.

If your home is in need to be painted, grab buckets, brushes, along with some overalls! You'll save money and unleash your artistic side! Picasso!

Create your own gym at home or basic equipment for exercise and leave joining a gym.

Find out the ways you could cut down on your expenses and make the most of your time. A suggestion you can make to yourself is to make the above list, along with any other list of DIY abilities you believe are worthy in your notebook. Then, mark off the skills you've mastered. Consider it an 'event calendar.

Imagine You're Like the Rich

Most interestingly, some of the most renowned minimalists are also its wealthiest inhabitants. Millionaires and billionaires often choose minimalist lifestyles to reduce expenses and develop a more frugal lifestyles. Here are some that might be beneficial to you:

Warren Buffett always comes to your mind when you think of the frugal billionaires. The primary point to be noted here is that one the most wealthy men on earth has opted out of living in a penthouse on the top of a tall building and is still living in the humble house which he purchased in the year 1958. Be sure that the roof above your head is in line with. If you're four members of a family and a house may be essential, but an extravagant mansion isn't. If you're an individual or two people, a one-bedroom apartment is all you need.

I've written previously about using public transport when you have the option. Ingvar Kamprad, who was the creator of IKEA was recognized for his use of public transportation , despite being billionaire and one of Europe's wealthiest men. If you are in an area that has great public transportation, you should make use of it whenever it is possible. Even better, if you reside in an area where it is easy to take a bike or walk to get there take advantage of it! By not driving, you save fuel costs, and if the area you live in doesn't require the purchase of an automobile, you can save thousands of dollars in the process of not having one!

Steve Jobs was a great minimalist as far as his clothes were about as well Mark

Zuckerberg carries on this style. Both businessmen wore an easy-to-wear uniform that simplified their decisions in life and exhibited their thriftiness. It is not necessary to adhere to the same uniforms however these examples will demonstrate how to not put too much importance on purchasing clothing from expensive and luxury brands.

Many of the people who are wealthy owe their success in the financial world to the principles of minimalism and frugality. Their associations with frugality and minimalism haven't diminished which is the factor that contributes into their financial stability. Learn these practices from the top!

Chapter Summary

* Make conscious choices regarding how you use your funds. Do you really need coffee each morning? Do you have the cash to purchase something other than coffee?

DIY projects to increase the amount you spend.

A lot of the wealthiest people around the globe have adopted minimalist principles. Learn from the top!

As you move on to the following chapter you'll discover that minimalism extends beyond the physical world, that time is the most important factor and that work do not need to be the primary goal of your life.

Chapter 5: Reclaim Your Time

Then, you'll discover how to make the most of your time by adopting the minimalist approach.

It's time for some work! You have discovered how to get rid of your home, organise your space and control your money and make smart purchases. Prior to learning about the next topic I'd like to encourage to encourage you to stop and make a plan for your minimalist lifestyle.

The Minimalist Plan

Get your notebook and pen and try to answer these questions. It may sound like a lot of work, but it will allow you to adopt a minimalist lifestyle and help train your brain to adapt to a minimalist lifestyle. A small amount of words for each question is enough.

* What are the reasons you would like to reduce your clutter?

* What are the worst habits that you have that you believe can be eliminated by a minimalist life style?

What improvements have I made to date and what is still needed to be done to make it better?

Another component to your minimalist plan is A Progress Log. This will be used to monitor your progress up to now. After you've completed the third question above, you'll be able to see what you want to do with the Progress Log.

Begin every Page of the Progress Log in the following manner:

* Note the date at the top.

Write a few words about your mood. Are you feeling calm, suffocated or neutral? What has minimalism done to you up to now?

Have you ever given away any items?

Have you bought anything?

What do you think you have cut down on? Habits of shopping, time spent doing things that are not productive, etc.

* What has changed or been improved? Have you more spare time? Have you saved up money for better activities?

The frequency of recording your Progress Log is entirely up to you, however I recommend recording each week once, either in the beginning or at the close each week. If the results seem to be gradual, you could increase the frequency to bimonthly or perhaps once per month. A Progress Log is a great method to assess how minimalism can improve your lifestyle, and also things that still need improvement.

Go Digital!

I have discussed digitizing printed material as a fantastic method to get rid of clutter. However, it is important to realize that decluttering does not just pertain to the physical realm. When we begin to move towards digitizing our files and important records, we should make sure that the digital spaces do not become overly cluttered. As we spend more time using computers and the Internet The possible clutter will impact our health just like the physical world. Be aware that you're an minimalist, as well. The quality and quantity of your online existence is just as important as the level of living within the real world.

These are steps for clean your hard drive and your cloud:

* Unsubscribe from newsletters and mailing lists. Each time we create an account on the internet, we choose to or inadvertently join their mailing lists. There could be a variety of newsletters that we have happily subscribed to since we believed the content would be beneficial to us or amuse us. How many newsletters do you go through? Many are in your inbox. Spend a few minutes of your schedule to unsubscribe from them.

Remove unnecessary documents and images. Did you save an interesting article that you found on the internet? Perhaps download a meme you enjoyed at one time? Your computer might be overloaded with these types of content and when they're not something you are viewing frequently then they ought to be removed.

* Remove any applications that are not used. Uninstall them and throw them away.

* Remove any unnecessary emails. This is a way to stop subscribing to newsletters and mailing lists. Once you've stopped any more emails from reaching you Go through your mailbox and delete any messages that are not necessary to use again.

Naturally, the digital world isn't limited to our laptops and computers. The digital world extends to the mobile device inside our pockets. We are addicted to our smartphones and we can cut down on our clutter and make more of our lives if we adopt a simple approach with our mobile phones and also.

Here are a few steps to using a phone that is minimalist:

Make use of your phone for its primary function: communication. I'm assuming you have an iPhone, which means that your phone isn't just used to make phone calls or compose messages in text. You go through entire films, look up your social media accounts, take photos as well as play games and even invest in the market. They can be an added convenience, and there's no need to delete all apps. But go through the apps you've not used in the past month and remove the ones you haven't used in a month.

Check out the applications you use and decide if it is worth making use of these apps. The ability to check your credit card and bank statements on your smartphone is extremely useful. If there's no reason to constantly check these accounts, you can delete the related applications. Do you really need to watch a whole film with your smartphone? Only if you're not an avid viewer on the plane. If social media management is your field of work and you must always be connected to a social media platform, remove those apps from your phone.

Make sure you regularly save your photos or videos onto your personal computer, to a cloud, or both. After that, erase all of them from your phone permanently. The same is true for audiobooks, podcasts, music as well as e-books.

• Remove the email account from your mobile. Also, if it's important to check your email regularly for reasons of academic or work, or you are constantly needing to access your email, you'll be required to keep the account. In the event that you don't, remove the accounts.

* Disable notifications. If it's not an emergency or for work-related reasons Do you require to be notified of each message or Facebook post, and every Instagram like?

Turn off your mobile completely, or silence it or switch off your mobile data. What are the times you've gone to a restaurant with a group of friends with the intention of on your smartphone than your companion? This might not be a good idea and you may have to be ready however, if you are able to consider one of these three alternatives so that you aren't distracted by your phone.

And let us not forget decluttering our Internet space! Are you finding that you Netflix list and YouTube "Watch later" list seem to be endless? Do you have an RSS reader full of numerous feeds that you don't recall ever subscribing? If you browse through your RSS reader it is likely that you won't be able to define the contents of every website in them. The Internet webspace is quite cluttered and could benefit from a minimal overhaul.

Let's start with your queue of media regardless of whether it's Netflix, Hulu, YouTube and any other of the other hundred streaming video websites. I'm pretty sure there are a plethora of video content in your queue that you'll "eventually" be able to view. Spend some time during your schedule and delete videos that you are certain you won't be able to watch.

A bit nervous I would browse the contents of my Netflix as well as Hulu queues and find an inventory of films that I didn't remember having added to my queue. I would look at the short reviews of these films, and then rack my head trying to recall the synopsis of the film that I was drawn to. If I didn't feel a strong urge to see the film it would be taken off the queue. In the event that the movie was popular and I could watch it anytime, either through a streaming service or by locating it in the library in my area and it was removed of the list.

This same principle is applicable for "Watch the video later" for YouTube as well as other websites similar to it. Maybe you should take the time to view the lengthy documentary or informative video. However, does the most recent cat video really need to be on your list? If you are a subscriber to an online channel, you may visit the channel's site anytime to view its videos . There's no need to put them on the "Watch for Later" list. If you have subscriptions, make sure to periodic clean-up. You'll be amazed at the number of YouTube channels you've signed up for on the spur of the moment. Maybe you were impressed by a particular video and thought that registering to the channel seemed like an natural next step. You might have signed up to the channel due to an interest or a need that you no longer need! Clean up!

Digital Social Life

Let's not forget about social media. us not overlook social media. Social media consumes a lot of our lives and, even without us realizing it it creates a lot of complexity in our lives. Since minimalism improves our lives through the power of simplicity, it's essential that we adopt the minimal approach to our different online platforms.

Let's begin with Facebook. How many friends do already have? More than one thousand? I am not sure but I'm sure that you have an enormous number of Facebook friends. It's possible that you don't realize it however, you're preventing yourself from living your ideal life due to this.

The first step is to look at your feeds on Facebook. Are there constantly negative posts from your Facebook acquaintances? I don't think so however it's very likely. If you're constantly receiving negative posts and they are frequently shared by the same people and groups, it might be time to delete them on Facebook. In absorbing the constant negative messages, you're adding to the chaos of life that you are aware of already is the opposite minimalistism. You can take this method of quitting unneeded Facebook groups, as well as the pages you don't follow that do not serve your needs and only make more clutter. Facebook is a platform that can be used to do a lot of things but it's mostly an opportunity to stay in contact with loved ones and friends. If you can, limit its use to this.

Similar to how I recommended using your phone for calling and texting, make sure you use Facebook to fulfill it's original function as often as you can. Spend time interacting with loved ones and not consuming endless videos. I've discussed how important freedom is to improve your quality of life. the moment you spend a lot of time is spent using social media, you have given up your freedom to indulge in more enjoyable activities that add more worth for your daily life.

I suggest applying the same approach across all the social networks. Check out your followers on Twitter and unfollow those who aren't worth your time or harm your life through their negative comments. On Instagram Are your following photographers with talent whose photos are a joy to look at because of their stunning beauty? Or are you following people with albums that are filled with endless selfies?

A professional site like LinkedIn is not without baggage. To connect and network it is commonplace to be open to invitations by any who has a connection with us. Even if they don't however, we might join them because we believe it could be beneficial professionally. Sooner or later, LinkedIn has become like Facebook! We get bombarded by unnecessary messages, we are prompted to wish a person a happy birthday or to praise them on their new job, and then we wonder who exactly is this person? We've become employees to our jobs and, consequently, potential connections that could be great additions to our social network. There's no reason to join with any and all of the people on LinkedIn Connect with the people who you interact with or collaborate with in your professional lives.

If you're an experienced marketer or not, we've all been caught by the numbers game that is played with social media. The amount of followers or connections, likes, thumbs up and so on. the number of followers, connections, likes, thumbs up, etc. to us greatly. Based on the situation the need to expand your audience through social media platforms to share the message or content to further our profession however, we should not let numbers dictate our decisions. The numbers in social media are in the same power as objects that exist in physical space. This is why we'll spend the money we earn to buy additional followers. We may even take to the extent of adhering to spam accounts promising to provide the user hundreds of followers. This kind of thinking can lead us to think of the real-world connection of a person worthy to be considered a Facebook friend, or the feeling that an acquaintance at a job event was more than welcome for you to add them into the LinkedIn network. A minimalist approach will teach that you should only try to get greater connections if required, and even you should not be taken for granted by numbers.

Digital Consumerism

Consumption is a major issue in physically-based environments, so too is the problem that is that is prevalent in the digital realm. A lot of your purchases could be made in the digital realm and it could be cyberspace that's costing you your freedom.

Consider for a moment whether any of these purchases are of interest to you:

* Music - Do you buy individual songs or purchase entire albums from a company like iTunes?

* Movies - Do you buy movies and have an electronic copy of the movie stored?

* Audiobooks and E-books

* Software and apps

* Games

Each of the above-mentioned purchases can increase the number on your bill , and possibly your credit card. Let's look at what we can do to adopt a minimal approach to these purchases made online. I will apply to the "If...then" principle However, I will propose a different solution:

* If you often buy music online, you ought to think about signing up to a music streaming service that lets you pay a

monthly cost and can access millions of songs you can stream unlimited. There are a variety of services that let you stream music at no cost, on an agreement that listen to an advertisement for a brief period before you are able to select another track. Whatever way you choose, you're saving money!

* If you often buy movies online, you should think about subscribing to streaming services such as Netflix as well as Hulu. Hulu also has a no-cost version with a huge selection of TV and film shows. If you don't need to watch a movie or TV show digitally look into whether the library in your area stocks DVDs.

For ebooks, there are a variety of digital libraries that permit users to "borrow" the book for a short period of period, similar to how you would do with the physical book from libraries. You can also consider an e-book subscription program and purchase a huge number of books at the cost of a monthly subscription; if you buy a lot of e-books and want to use them all, this will be more economical. With audiobooks, you can find options like Audible which allow you to download one book for free each month, for a monthly cost. In addition, the monthly subscription is a discount on additional books. This is something you should look at if you buy audiobooks often. Additionally, if you're looking for an audiobook of books that are that is in the public domain (meaning that the copyright for it expires) go to www.Librivox.org and similar sites. They have audiobooks available for a variety of books in the public domain, ranging from the Aesop Fables to the work from Geoffrey Chaucer.

* Software and apps aren't always easy to navigate. There are many available for free that we can download without hesitation. As I've already mentioned make sure you clear your devices of all unwanted software and apps. What happens to the ones you bought? There are two options to this issue. If there's an app or program that you'd like to purchase you should first search for an alternative that is free.

Consider "Do I require an app to film videos with my phone or is the built-in app adequate?" This leads to the other option of consider whether you truly require the app. In the same way There are numerous excellent apps that enhance the quality of videos you take using your smartphone. The apps have been utilized to create feature films! If you're not a professional filmmaker or do not have the desire to produce cinema quality videos, there's no need to buy this application. Make sure you save your money so you can have the flexibility to create something else!

* If you're planning to buy a game I'd like you to take the time for it! Be sure to dedicate time playing this game. It is not necessary to play for a long time but what's the point of spending money on the game if you'll not play it? There is the difference between buying games that are video and an easy game to play using your mobile. Games designed for phones are intended for filling up the time - for instance, during lunch or during our commute. If this is the reason you enjoy

games on your smartphone, take a look at free games that can fill your time and be enjoyable to play. Find alternative ways to fill up the time that isn't being used - there was a time that we didn't have to put our heads on our phones in order to have fun minutes of unoccupied time!

This is the simplest method of buying digital items. Find these alternatives to save cash on purchases made online and cut down on your use of digital devices. Limiting your digital use can improve your quality of life.

Time and Time Yet...

Time is the most important factor! The primary goal and purpose of living a minimalist life is to make sure you have more time and flexibility to pursue your goals in your life. The freedom and time you have will ensure that you live your life to the fullest. It's only when the time is taken away from us that we start to appreciate the value of it for our life. When you have time to spare or you've previously had it, it's not difficult to fall into the trap of minimalism and fall into trap of excessive consumption, which can be dangerous to your freedom and time. Many people opt for minimalism when they realize that their time and freedom has lost to their lives. You have discovered how an act such as a purchase of a few dollars can impact your freedom and time at a later time. This is the reason monitoring and managing your time is an important part of becoming an effective minimalist.

It's time to grab your pen and notebook again! Here's what I want you to note down:

What freedom and time do you think you've lost? Are you missing the holidays, special events or important purchases over the long term?

* What kind of time and freedom have you gained through the minimalist lifestyle? Think about an action that was minimalist that brought you advantages, for instance you could consider spending less on

materials and consequently you took that vacation in The Bahamas!

This is the time to look at your time. Ideally , you'll be spending most of your time in leisure however this isn't always feasible. School, work, and the demands of life will likely be the primary focus and will be a major part all of your day. But, it is important to ensure that they don't consume all your time, and that you're able to enjoy plenty of time that is spent on things you would like to do!

Keep your notebook and pen at your side. On a blank paper note "Time Log" at the topof the page, with the date below it. Note a specific day of your week on your Time Log. Note how much time was dedicated to school, work and other responsibilities. It can be recorded by following the format:

* Gym session from 6 AM until 7 9 (1 hour)

* Breakfast with friends between 7:30 and 8:30 AM (1 hour)

* Hours of work: 9 AM until 5 8 PM (8 hours)

* Attending class and studying from 7 pm to 9 9:00 PM (2 hours)

* Chores at various times throughout the day. (Total accumulation: 1 Hour)

* Rewatching my most-loved television show, 10 PM-11 midnight (1 Hour)

Your total time spent for the day was 14 hours. There were 10 hours left and some of it would likely be spent sleeping. If you can sleep for eight hours, that's 2 hours left. It could be spread out across an entire day, but it will not be a continuous 2 hours. What are you doing in those two hours? This example indicates that study, work and chores take up most part of your day. While this isn't a surprise however, the amount of time you have to do the things you really want to do is very limited. Are you able to squeeze in an extended workout? Instead of just eating breakfast with your friends would you like to spend the whole time with them? and catch up with your favourite TV show? I'm sure you'd like to watch it in a binge!

Let's look at learning and attending classes first. It could be necessary to attend a live class If you're in a university or taking a professional development class look into options to attend these classes on the internet. You will be able to take more time to complete the course, and not be forced to attend an auditorium for a certain duration. While studying, determine what methods will allow you to learn in a more efficient way. So, studying will take much less time, but not affecting your performance in the exam or project. If your study involves the reading of a large amount of text Here are some strategies you can employ to comprehend the text better:

• Take a speed-reading class This will not just enable you to read more quickly and more efficiently, but also to be able to absorb information faster.

Check if there are any notes that are summarized for your book. If you're required to read a novel as part of an academic course, check whether there are any publications or notes online that provide the main aspects that the story. The more popular it is the higher chances.

* Reading instead of listening! If your text is accessible in the form of an audiobook, this might be the most efficient method of understanding the text. It is also easy to revisit a particular part with an audiobook than go back and forth through pages of the text.

* Make an study group. If you study alongside others and bounce ideas off of each other, you'll be able to comprehend the text faster and reduce the amount of study you will need to complete for the best results.

What about those nagging chores, errands, or obligations we all throw at us? They can hinder our studies and work and even our time off. Can we cut down the amount of time we spend on these essentials and increase our time for leisure activities?

The requirements for these will be constantly changing and you should take a few minutes to write down your chores, errands and tasks you need to take on every day. Here's an example:

* Drop the children to school early in the morning, and take them back at the end of the day.

Make sure that all bills are paid and there aren't any outstanding or unpaid charges.

* Make sure washing is completed and there is enough clothing to last the next day.

* Ensure there is enough food available to last the duration of the day.

Let us now employ minimalism to tackle these issues and maximise our time.

* Continue dropping off your child to school each morning. Then return them at the end of the day. There should be no change here as long as you are able to. If you truly need alternatives, look into whether you can carpool or school buses

or another form of public transportation that takes children on and off school.

To eliminate the stress of constantly checking your bills to see if they require payment, consider the possibility of setting up an automatic payment schedule to pay the bills. Make sure you have enough money in all times! A lot of automatic payment systems notify you that your account will be due soon which means you'll be able to make adjustments if needed.

If you're a minimalist you'll need a small wardrobe, which means you will require laundry more frequently than if you were a closet with clothes. Most of the time, the best time to dry and wash your clothes is in the evening to ensure they're prepared for the next day. If you want to iron, consider whether you can schedule some time in the evening or early in the morning or during your free time.

Try to cook food ahead. If you can prepare meals in bulk, you can cut down or completely eliminate the need to cook on a weekday.

By taking these simple steps, you can let you have more time in your working week. These are just a few small steps towards maximising your time. What about the bigger one? Work!

Work

The reduction of the hours you work isn't an easy task and you might not be able to achieve it. However, if you're in a position to clear some other areas of your life and create time for relaxation, your the work you do will not be overwhelming. There are a few things to think about when you're able to decrease the amount of time you devote to your work:

* Do you have to work the amount of hours? Do you prefer to work these hours? Are you working longer times to cover your debt?

Are you prepared to switch jobs or profession to find one that is more convenient for your lifestyle even if it results in a lower wage?

Are you working too much to get a promotion or simply for creating a brand?

Are you obliged to work a particular amount of hours per week? It could be that it is true but you're voluntarily making the decision to work more hours. You don't have to settle any outstanding debt, and you have more than enough funds to cover your expenses. What do you have in mind in the meantime? If you're saving to purchase something It is time to re-read and examine the purchase that is coming up.

Does the investment make sense? If you're buying a brand new home for your family members, I'd say yes. The same applies to a car for instance, if you require a car to travel regularly. Maybe the money earned is used to put into investing in the future. If you're working extra hours to take a vacation then it's worth the effort! But are you saving for items that you can't afford? or to be able to budget for Black Friday as well as Christmas shopping? It's not worth the extra time - cut down on your work time. If the purchase is worthwhile, you must be sure that after the purchase has been made, you can reduce your working hours to be able to enjoy the purchase. If the extra hours are for paying off your debt, continue working! Make sure that when the debt is paid off, you get some time off. In the end, you're looking to become debt free so that you have more freedom and time for you.

What if you're in a position to decrease the hours you are working? Perhaps you're required to work a certain amount of hours, or perhaps you're required to be working overtime, and have no hope of having your hours cut. Are you ready to change jobs? Are you considering a shift to a different firm that allows you to work for a smaller amount of hours? Perhaps you could find a job in a different field that will require a cut in pay? What about taking the largest leap of all and creating your own business? These are tough decisions, and if you're considering one or more of them, I urge you to be patient and take into account the advantages and disadvantages of your choices.

Changes in your job within your workplace could mean less hours, however it may not be in an area you enjoy or are proficient in. A new job or job might guarantee you a lower number of hours. However, should it result in the prospect of a lower pay, it could result in additional issues. Perhaps it's harder to pay off your debts and pay off your debt, or even make worthwhile purchases. There may be more time for relaxation however you might not have enough money to fund some of your leisure activities. Perhaps your vacation will have to be delayed for a long time. If you are a parent, this could be very difficult. You would not wish to be deprived of any benefit due to a smaller pay.

There are those who are minimalists and have opted to change careers with a lower pay and have found it to be beneficial. Although you might not make a profit on certain items, if you adhere to a minimalist lifestyle, you might not require the extra money. Perhaps everything you require is paid for by your new income and you also have the time to do these activities.

How do you go about getting an increase in rank? Promotions and "moving upwards" always seem to be the next natural step. We are taught to constantly step outside of our comfort zones and always strive to do the best we can Keep our options open and never ever stop moving. However, this is the trap that we fall into, and it's quite similar to the way we fall into the trap of consumption. Try to keep it simple when getting promoted - take a look at what the promotion can bring you. Most likely , it will provide you with more prestige and a better status as well as a greater pay. However, is it also giving your more flexibility and freedom? Be aware of the reason you're working more hours and whether or not a promotion is worth the effort even if it doesn't improve your life quality.

Another reason why we want to do more work or get promotions is because of the status. There is nothing different between our hoarding and consumption of goods and possessions, as well as our desire to maintain appearances by working too much. Our culture and society wants us to project the image of being working and busy. The notion of having time to relax is viewed as a source of guilt when we tell people, "They have too much time to do," it is an insult, not being a compliment!

You are an minimalist! Your goal is to live your life more simply. Although others might not be able to comprehend your choices and actions but you shouldn't work just to maintain the appearance. You're not a minimalist just to make others feel special; the reason you're a minimalist is who wants to improve your existence for your self. Don't forget this!

Maintaining Minimalist

For a final thought I would like to emphasize the dangers of breaking from the minimalist mindset and getting sucked into consumerism , which leads to excessive spending and reckless living. Consider for a moment about the reasons you chose to go through this book and to learn about the concept of minimalism. Take out your notebook for a second time and write an outline (as brief or long as you'd like) of the reasons you chose to study minimalism. Here are a few common motives, and I'm sure one, many, or all of them are applicable to you.

* Simplifying your life

* Saving money by spending less. your money

* Repaying the debt

* Living a more deliberate and deliberate way of life

* Eliminating digital and physical clutter

This is a difficult practice. Below your reasons for wanting to become a minimalist make the reasons that prevented you from becoming minimalist earlier. Consider, why did I continue to have these habits prior to which are contrary to minimalism?

Here are a few reasons why people are not minimalists:

* Aversion to consumption products, whether they are material or food, drugs or other.

Feeling that spending brings joy and increases the quality of your life

* Societal expectations

If you look at the two lists, you can see the things that have changed and what needs to be changed - if at all. Maybe you were addicted to consumption but now it has been cured. Do you at times think you'd be more content if you had more items? It's not easy to achieve minimalism over night; it takes some time for the habits and emotions to grow. Be patient and not in a hurry. If you do the exercises in this book, you will see it happen.

What are the expectations of society? This is perhaps the most important reason for why people aren't minimalists, even though they are innately inclined to live a minimalist way of life. I decided to keep this idea for the last moment, since this is something to think about as you consider your path towards living a minimalist lifestyle.

A lot of people who reside in the richest and most developed nations around the globe become entangled in consumption due to pressures from society. Most of the time, wealthy nations show their wealth by displaying what its citizens have and have. Many people living in these countries are constantly reminded of their wealth through pictures and figures of people from less developed nations. Photos of children who don't have shoes are displayed, as are images of the shabby housing for families, or those who walk for miles because they do not have access to cars. This can lead to the perception that, because of our possessions and the access to more items that we enjoy a better standing in the world. This attitude weighs on our shoulders all through our lives. To demonstrate our achievements in our lives, we should have more space in our homes or a better car and a variety of things including designer clothes to antique furniture to books that we would never read but are popular and therefore the display of our intelligence. Being able to live up to this ideal is a social pressure, and that is the reason why we don't live well-planned and measured lives that is the foundation for the minimal lifestyle based on.

What about people who live in "developing" countries? It's not as obvious but they're facing the same social pressures as those living who live in "First Third World" nations are facing. Their economies are expanding and, as a consequence the income of their inhabitants is rising dramatically. To celebrate this new income, the inhabitants of developing countries are spending. First time ever ever, they're wearing designer clothes or perhaps buying their first automobile or upgrading their existing vehicle to a more expensive. The empty spaces within their homes fill up in the span of a few days likely due to a recently discovered an almost instant appreciation of art and sculpture. Due to the high-speed consumption they face and the pressure to be busy, they might feel that life is improving and they're happier. It's possible that they are! In the end, they're not as devoid of possessions like they were prior to. But eventually, they will discover that possessions don't bring them real satisfaction. A new wave of minimalism could be seen in these countries in the near future.

You don't need to be This To Be Strenuous...

A lot of us have been taught the concept of working harder to make more money. We are taught that hard work is the most important thing. But, working smartly is often undervalued. Minimalism doesn't want you to turn money into the main goal of your life, but recognizes that it's an essential aspect of living so a continuous, high-earning lifestyle and earning a good income is essential for many people. If you are in the category of having to earn more money in order to support a certain life style or to provide for those around you, there could be methods to cut back on your hours without sacrificing your financial gain. Here are some of them:

* Get help for your work. This might sound counter to the self-help lifestyle that was discussed previously, But remember that this is in fact for your work. Are there any tasks that can be delegated to someone else? There is a chance that you are doing something that isn't productive however it may increase productivity. The work that is completed will increase and, consequently the financial benefits could be. If, for instance, you require writing tasks completed There are a variety of websites like Fiverr.com which for of as little as $5, you can get these services done. It's not an enormous amount of money and you'll have an experienced professional who can perform better than you do, which means you can reap more profits.

* Automation! It is evident that automation doesn't perform for all jobs However, there might be methods you can follow to automate some aspects of your work. The process of automating your work may be long however it offers the benefit of a bargain. A lot of Internet entrepreneurs will create an item and then programme it to ensure the Artificial Intelligence manages the work that humans normally perform. The work they do is significantly reduced, while the item continues to earn them profits. Find out if there's something in your work that you can automate.

Make sure you're as well-informed as you can be in all other aspects of your job to ensure maximum efficiency. This is especially important when you run a business. A department in your company might be deliberately completing the work on a more extended schedule and, therefore, overcharging you or you may find the most efficient method to finish the job.

Earn multiple income sources. Have you ever heard someone saying, "I want to do this, but I'll not earn a lot of cash!" or "I want to do that, but unfortunately I won't make an enormous amount of cash!" But who says that your main occupation should be the only source of income? Research ways you can create several streams of income through a second job performing odd-jobs in which you're proficient at or investing your money and so on. Don't think that your field should hinder flexibility in your finances.

Human beings to seek out and use spare time to consider what is most important to us. Don't forget that this book is all about the idea of living a minimalistic lifestyle. it has talked about how to rid oneself of all things, ways to cut costs and control one's financial affairs. However, the main goal of these goals involves living a fulfilling life. It's deliberate positive, meaningful, and joyful living that is the standard for a high-quality life. Be aware of this throughout your ongoing journey to minimalistism.

This is the time for another exercise in reflection; go to your notebook and pen time and try to take the time to answer these questions the greatest detail you can:

What made you decide to purchase this book to discover the concept of the concept of minimalism? (I realize this question was asked before, however, your perspective will shift as you progress on the journey.)

* What steps did you take to be minimalist?

What steps were most simple to follow?

What were the steps that were most difficult to complete?

What are the steps you need to do in order to remain a minimalist?

* Are there any actions that you are unable to or will not undertake?

* What reaction did other people feel when you announced that your commitment to a minimalist way of life?

Did you face any criticism? Do you have a defense for yourself? And what did you do?

* What is the most rewarding aspect of becoming minimalist?

* What is the most painful aspect of becoming minimalist?

It may seem long and unimportant at this point, as you're near the final chapter however, I'd suggest you to pay attention to the questions above and revisit the questions from time to time. Perhaps you can create a plan of each month at least every three months, when you'll go over the questions and try to answer the questions again.

Chapter Summary

* The digital age consumes a lot of our lives, but it doesn't necessarily have to be this way.

* A minimalist who is a master of his craft knows something or two regarding time management.

* Work to your schedule. Your schedule shouldn't interfere with your work.

In the next chapter you'll learn about the quality of life and how it connects to minimalism.

Chapter 6: Quality Of Life

This chapter you'll be taught about the importance of the importance of quality of life and why it is important to value your peace of mind.

We all surrender to our heart's desires, do you not? Whatever our current situation or the surroundings that we were raised in, we are afflicted with an overwhelming sense of unsatisfaction. Every person has the desire to accomplish something, or perhaps, even more so to achieve something. This is why we tend to indulge in. We didn't grow up with an item, but when we have the money to buy it, we don't hesitate to purchase it.

Our needs and our expectations of living alter, and for the majority of us, the cost of living continues to rise. We wish to find an employment with a specific amount of money and believe that once we have reached the point of no return, our life is established and there is nothing to be concerned about. But, as our living standards improve and we get used to it.

In time, we start to get over it. We never felt satisfied with the conditions in which the children were brought up, no matter the level of privilege it could have been. consequently we longed for more. This is the same with our lifestyle as we feel it's not enough and, as a result we seek out more. Progress is a great word but we don't really understand what that signifies. While we should aim to achieve the highest quality of life however, we shouldn't be able to confuse it with the quality of life.

What is the meaning of quality of life? You've heard the term many times in this book. Before you proceed in your minimalist path I'd like you to have a clear knowledge of what it means. Quality of life refers to the happiness a person is experiencing throughout their lives. The good things in their lives outweigh the negatives, and they generally have an overall sense of satisfaction and joy. Our progress is dependent on the purchase of material things and we're so obsessed with these things that we believe that, no matter what we already have we are yet to be able to enjoy what we need to be happy.

The most painful part is that once we have these items of material possession and lose them, it's not unusual to end up losing what was already bringing us joy. To sustain our new lifestyles we must endure a long and hard day, often at the expense of other activities that are more enjoyable so we don't miss the chance to increase our earnings. Sooner or later our lives are consumed by pursuing happiness instead of enjoying life and doing what we are passionate about, with those whom we cherish. This is a trap we have all fell into and the worst part is that a lot of us are only able to recognize it at a later stage. However, I would like to assure you that it's never too late to make making a shift.

There is a common misconception how one of the most common misconceptions about minimalism is the lifestyle is just for certain demographics that includes the conditions is that one must be of certain age to be able to enjoy the minimalist lifestyle. Whatever your age or what stage of your life you are able to live a minimalist lifestyle if like to. There is a chance of backlash, but the majority of it is misunderstanding. If you declare your intention to go minimalist will be a turn of heads and many will think that you want to be an ascetic. Be patient and don't overdo it trying to convince people that what you're doing is true. Don't attempt to preach to them either. keep in mind that minimalism isn't an ideology.

You're doing this to yourself. You are conscious of your lifestyle and have the desire to live your life more mindfully and live your life with a sense of purpose. This is the reason you've took the decision to step and live your life with the idea of minimalism. As a concept and an approach to life the concept of minimalism has been around for centuries and has been found in various forms throughout diverse styles from the East to the West. One common element that can be seen in all the different minimalism schools is a specific set of values that are considered to be suitable to lead a tranquil life. Peace of mind is the goal for everyone Self-help is increasing due to the lack of calm. The recent enthusiasm for minimalism also been triggered by the fact that people are who are stressed out, and having a difficult time finding tranquility. You've heard about trade-offs. Should buy this product? What's the price? Do you have the time and flexibility when you buy a product?

As a final test you should take your notebook and tear out one page (you might need multiple pages) Answer these questions with as many specifics as you can.

* Before you begin your journey of minimalism which were the three most serene and enjoyable moments in your life? Define these moments as precisely as you can.

* Before you begin your journey of minimalism which were the three most

enjoyable moments in your life? Define these moments as clearly as you can.

* Before you begin your journey to minimalism, which were the three most difficult moments in your life? Be as specific as you can.

Once you've written them and framed, put them on the wall. You can put them on a tape, place them on the wall. Just make sure that the writing is visible on a wall that you often see on a daily basis. You must strive to make sure that your choices will bring peace of mind and satisfaction; and does not cause discomfort. Let's take a look to some of the "If...then" sentences. After you've learned this technique, it's appropriate to put three requirements on the. After you have asked the if then, you should ask yourself "Will I then be rewarded with pleasure, peace or suffering?"

Ideally, you will find satisfaction and peace simultaneously. It's not always the case however, you should strive every day to find peace. If you can maintain a calm mind, pleasure will flow naturally. However, enjoyment may not always be the best way to achieve peace of mind and it can sometimes cause suffering. Consumption is a source of pleasure. There is a feeling of instant satisfaction whenever we purchase an item we have put in so much effort in our jobs to achieve. We look forward to the presents we'll receive to celebrate our birthdays or an occasion like Christmas We are overwhelmed when we get the present that we would like.

However, eventually the tangible goods can give us peace of mind. The enjoyment fades away and we might actually be in a lot of pain due to the tangible good. This is also true of our dream job. Many of us believe that if we're able to achieve everything we wish for that we have found satisfaction. We are unhappy if we don't get everything we want or have put in a lot of effort to achieve. Here's an interesting idea: maybe not getting everything we desire is the definition of freedom.

Although I don't want you to give up on your dreams or feel like you have to be happy throughout the day, you shouldn't be basing your satisfaction on circumstances. No matter if you succeed or fail to achieve the pursuit of a goal, you will feel content. If you're in calm and take pleasure in life's moments, then it's a sure sign that you've achieved your liberty. Make every effort to maintain this. This is the aim of minimalism. I am sure that by doing the exercises provided in this book, you will succeed in achieving the things you really want in your life. Your perspective will shift, and you'll be living your the rest of your life with a greater awareness. Your life won't be governed by the possessions you own and you will appreciate every item you have and the ones you'll have in the near future.

What you've achieved to date is an important achievement. Don't be concerned when you believe there is much more to be accomplished. Your successes thus far indicate that you are on the right track; you have shown an intense sense of dedication and you are able to continuing to be an individual who lives a minimalist lifestyle. The minimalist lifestyle can be an uphill climb, but you've demonstrated tremendous bravery as well as I wish you success in the journey.

Chapter Summary

* We're so obsessed with raising our standards life that we neglect the quality of our lives.

* Do not underestimate the importance of the peace of mind.

Make sure that your actions leave you with peace of mind as well as satisfaction.

Chapter 7: Creating A Budget

A budgeting process can prove to be challenging, particularly in the event that you've never attempted it before. The most important thing to do is begin, and you'll notice that as you write down your income and expenses then the other things will flow through your head. The document doesn't have to be perfect right from the beginning and you can always add or remove things.

To make an effective budget that is able to adapt to your needs it is essential to be aware of your objectives. If you don't have any intention of having savings accounts and believe it's useless, then what's the purpose to have a certain percentage of your budget devoted to saving? If we take a scenario that isn't so extreme as this one If you don't have or require a car, it's not logical to include it in your budget. However , you should consider the amount you spend on transportation and put it in the category of transportation.

Examine the information you have from the previous months and then work to the next step with the help of your objectives. If you don't have any clue as to the exact amount of money you've spent over the last few months, request the bank to provide you with a credit card or debit card report that includes all the things you've spent your money on. Although this may be a bit uncomfortable to see (specially in the event that you've spent an enormous amount of money on things that aren't worth it) but it can allow you to open your eyes to what's happening regarding your financial situation.

Begin by using your earnings as your first base.

Be aware that your income must be sufficient to be sufficient to:

Costs

Savings

Investments (or savings for investing)

Repayments for debt

The amount you choose to allocate to each of these categories is completely on your personal preferences.

When you've got an idea of the amount of how much you're willing to invest in expenses each month, then you are able to start to plan your budget.

The first step is to add the necessary expenses that you are unable to get rid of and will need to pay each month like rent, car payment fuel and insurance, food, etc.

You will now have some extra cash that you can put to purchase the things you'd like to have such as a brand new jacket or morning coffee (which aren't really necessary but add to your overall satisfaction).

If you take a close examine the things you're spending money on, you might decide to alter some of your habits. The newly cash can be put to your savings account or go towards something more meaningful to you like having enough money to go to the theatre each month or even funding your account for trading to begin trading on the market. This is likely depend on your goals since those who want to be an artist will spend their cash in a completely different fashion as compared to someone who hopes to become an investor.

BUDGETING TOOLS and TECHNIQUES

In the end , it's about finding the system that is right for you. It may be the most ideal system to budget, but If it doesn't suit you, then you're unlikely to stick with it, which means you'll end up exactly at the point you began, which is not paying attention to your financials.

System of envelopes

This one is very interesting and I decided to test it as it caught my interest. It involves segregating your money into several envelopes that have different categories on them, like "rent", "food", "gas", "savings" and so on. The main purpose behind this process is to have an amount that is designated for each of the envelopes. You then only use that money in. If you're unable to find funds within one envelope you must "steal" money from other ones to cover that one. That will require you to figure out how to divide your funds.

Although I didn't end up making this my sole method however, I did find myself applying this system on my saving. If I'm looking to save money for travel, a brand new phone, or even to keep money that I cannot spend, I make use of envelopes.

The great thing with envelopes is that you can write on them and keep a an eye on how much you've got on the inside. Every one of my envelopes is labeled with the aim I'm hoping to accomplish using it and the amount I'll need , as well as a motivational quote on how to save money which I check every time I look at the envelope.

Excel

The process is pretty simple, just enter your expenses and income, then determine the amount you're spending. If you're able to come up with a positive number after subtracting the cost of your expenses from your earnings then you're doing well. Increase that number and you save money each month. The benefit for using Excel is that it allows you to create a spreadsheet which you can cut and paste each month to see what you're doing. In addition, you don't require an calculator because you can insert the formula directly on the spreadsheets.

This is another method I prefer since it's very simple and you can secure the document using an encryption key so only you are able to view it.

Excel is by far my most used method since it's easiest and can help you organize all the details by simplifying processes.

Apps

There are a number of fantastic budgeting applications available that automatically connect to your debit and credit cards to allow you to have a clear overview of the way you're spending your money. There are a few of them: Mint, You Need a Budget and Wally.

70/20/10

If you've been reading the novel The Richest Man in Babylon it will be a familiar story to you. In the text, author advises that you spend 70% of your expenditure (in this case, it's clothing and any other luxury that you might wish to grant yourself) 20% in order to settle any outstanding debts you may have and 10 percent to save. The trick is to save until you reach a level where you are able to put that money to work. Be sure to only invest in things that you're comfortable with or you are familiar with. It's a costly investment in the event that you lose the cash.

50/30/20

It's a bit like the 70/20/10 model, but in this case, you pay 50% on essentials like rent, heating and food, and 30 percent on desires like clothing or cable, and 20 percent on savings and the repayment of debt.

Whatever you decide to do, ensure that you are congruous with your choice and avoid using incorrect information because the only person you'll lie to is yourself.

Make use of a system that works with your personality If you're required to be reminded to complete the input for your expenses each month, you can set an alarm on your mobile every 5th of each month. You should also have a document where you can maintain your budget easily accessible.

Smart Budget

To create an effective budget it is essential to be aware of the amount you spend and where exactly is your money going every month. It's not necessary to keep track of it each month, as you could get lost in noting down every gum packet, but you'll know where your money goes and how you can control it prior to spending it. Instead of keeping track of $1.50 for coffee each month, you can simply estimate the amount you spend on coffee as well as other meals in general , and then assign it to your food group. This is a way to skip the hassle of calculating the cost of your morning coffee every day. It will give you an average of the number of drinks you consume multiplied by the days you typically drink coffee. While this isn't the most exact method, it can make a huge difference in time that you can utilize to pursue other pursuits that generate income, regardless of whether they are income-generating things or just time spent with your family members.

A well-planned budget can allow you to quickly assess the direction of your money and to know what you can conserve and invest. It's a method to turn an "boring" budgeting method into something you can utilize every month and comprehend the entire process in only 5 minutes. It's not time-consuming and everything is automated. The result? easily trackable financials.

A good budget starts with the premise that you're trying to earn more cash, live within your budget and build up your wealth. At the same time, you must cutting down on high-interest debt and repaying loans.

Summarized:

INCOME

To increase this, you should do so by acquiring assets that give you a new stream of income each month. The increase in your income will allow you to accumulate more assets, making your earnings increase exponentially, rather than linearly like it would be with a typical job.

The trick to keep this process as easy as you can is to take the time to make an Excel sheet, and then include all sources that you're receiving funds. If you're looking to add a new source, it's as easy as adding one more row, and Excel will add it all up automatically with formulas included in each cell.

Example of Income Sources

The Job is 9-5 (could be Half-time job) $1,800

Freelancing $150

YouTube $120

Stock photos $0.25

eBook royalties $77

Total Income $2,147.25

COSTS

Reduce your expenses if you can, or when you're spending more each month than what you're making. A simple way to cut down your expenses is to take all the stuff that's not beneficial to you or isn't making a difference to your well-being or happiness. If your income is increasing, ensure that your expenses don't rise by the same percentage. The most straightforward thing to do is automate the essential payments along with the contributions to your investment or savings accounts.

Example of Expenses

Rent (automated) - - $800

Utilities (automated) (included)

Food $200 for food

Food out/ Coffee $130

Auto Payment: $180

Gas $120

Car insurance is $60

Entertainment - $60

Total Costs - $1,550

TOTAL: INCOME - Expenses: $597.25

In the example from this instance, your earnings surpasses your expenses. This is great because you can put the rest to invest or save.

If your total was negative then you must discover a way to make it positive since having a negative figure can lead to debt since you're paying more than you earn.

Now, let me take a look at your finances as if you were a corporation or business. In addition to the revenue you earn and the costs you must incur businesses, there are both liabilities and assets. It's not that different from the way our financial system.

ASSETS

Assets are valuable and can make you money each month, so it's a good idea to invest in and increase your assets.

Car $5,000

Jewellery $500

Stocks $2,000

Cash $990

Total $8,490

LIABILITY

The liabilities are all you owe. They make money out of you, lower them unless they contribute to your overall health and happiness.

Car loan - $2,800

Credit card debt: $1,800

Total $4,600

NET WORTH

Another important number to know is the net worth. This is the amount of your assets against what you owe, and it can help you know how much you're earning.

NET WORTH: ASSETS - LIABILITIES: $8,490 - $4,600

TOTAL NET WORTH: $3,890

Debt can cost you many times the amount due is pushing your net worth to the red line. Similar to your budget, you must try to build an income that is positive.

Wealth is an illusion

Would you respond if said that you might be living the life of the wealthy right now? and that the majority of people who live extravagant lifestyles are financially strained or even in debt? Be careful about the people admire and make you wish that you could have their lifestyles, as the majority of people are in debt to afford this lifestyle. Even if you earn an annual salary of $250,000 and spending $275,000 per year, you're less valuable (financially in the sense of net worth) than someone making $50,000 per year and only saving half and is not in debt. As a high income earner, you'll have the benefit that by changing your routines, you could save a lot more money in a shorter amount of time than the one who earns only $50,000.

Let's take a look at an example:

Derek is just a teenager and is an executive in a hotel and earns $50,000 after tax but he is living with parents, and isn't married and doesn't have children. The monthly income after taxes approximate: $ 4,167.

Bruce is a senior engineer in data engineering and earns $ 150,000 a year after taxes. He has 3 kids as well as a wife named Angela who has decided to leave her job to be able to look after their children. (If you're a woman and would prefer Angela as the chief data engineer , then you can imagine it in that manner). Income after taxes approximately $12,500.

Because Derek is a child of his parent, he is able to pay nothing to pay for other than the cellphone charge ($60) and offered to pay for the electric charge ($112) to support his family. The family lives out in suburbs of an apartment that his parents purchased after they were married. He loves going out with his buddies once per week to a good dining establishment ($400) and also going out to clubs each week ($550). Additionally the coffee he purchases ($90) each morning, and he eats lunch ($357) on the job every day as his break doesn't last long enough to get back to his home. He is able to save the rest of his money since he would like to travel around the world and invest in the future.

The expenses of Derek's month: $1,569

The savings of Derek per month: $2,598

Derek's annual savings projections is $ 31,176

Bruce's circumstance is slightly different. He must pay rent on a five bedroom home that costs $4,050 per month . This is in addition to every expense associated with having a house, including the electric bill ($180) and water. Water is included, unless you exceed your water allowance. Everyone living in the house, except for their youngest daughter is connected to phones ($60 plus 4 = 244) and they are also required to pay their internet bills ($100) as well as cables ($120) as well as organic meals ($1,600).

Additionally, he has a loan for his brand new car ($600) in addition to his wife's ($450) for both which he must cover car insurance ($180).

Two of his sons are currently in high school and attend private primary school ($1,735.50) as well as his child is in the preschool ($416).

Other expenses include clothes each month for everyone of the household ($600) in addition to Angela enjoys luxury handbags and other items ($450).

Bruce has also made the decision that he wanted to go with his entire family on vacation to Italy for his kids to meet their aunts and uncles as Angela has a family of

Italian and she wanted to see her relatives. because he holds a higher interest rate credit card, he determined to pay at least two thousand dollars per month.

Bruce's expenses per month: $ 12,721.50

Bruce's deficit per month: -$ 221.50

Bruce's annual deficit projections$ 2,658

You're better off being wealthy rather than appear wealthy. The majority of "rich" people have debts since they must finance the highest standard of living in order to look good. The problem is that you're not able to earn the lifestyle you're living. In the earlier example, it didn't need to be a problem that Bruce was earning nearly 3 higher than Derek due to his large expenses that he wound in spending more than he earned. In the end, Derek's savings might be used to purchase an investment property which would give an income that is semi-passive which allows his to be able to retire sooner. But, if Bruce realizes that he's been living an unhealthy life that's putting his family and himself in debt, and decides to alter his lifestyle, then it could be possible to make the same change.

Start by earning it first, then do it and live it. You'll realize that the things you thought you wanted initially was not really what you were looking for it was more of an assumption about what you're expected attain by a certain point in our lives. Do not be pressured by other people to accept an unsatisfactory job which you think is hurting you simply due to the fact that it's an "amazing possibility".

There's also a way to live a luxurious life that most people aren't aware of and that is that you can be a millionaire and still not being able to earn as much as one. Many countries where prices of life are much lower than the U.S., meaning that with the same amount of money you can live like the king of those countries. There is one city located in Guatemala named Antigua that has a large proportion of homeowners with retirement age Americans. Do you have a clue what the reason is? In addition to being a gorgeous city, it's also incredibly affordable relative to America which means that even if you were to retire and receive the monthly payments, even if they weren't enough to support the standard that you were able to enjoy in Chicago however, you could be able to enjoy a comfortable life for many years to be in Antigua. If you were to one of neighbouring cities in Guatemala which are more expensive than Antigua in comparison, you'll likely be unable to sustain an existence there even if you're employed all day in that town or city. What can we learn from of this? It's best to earn a good income, but live within your means, regardless of whether it is working from home and living in a less expensive area like Thailand with stunning views. or even shifting to a less expensive place within your country, city, or cutting down on your expenses and living within your budget regardless of where you may be.

THE STARTING POINT YOU CHOOSE DOES NOT IMPLY the outcome

Did you remember the elephant that was born? It's true that we all begin somewhere. It doesn't matter that you only completed high school or did not complete your college. The people who continue to put in the time and effort to the right places will be recognized for the service they provide. It also means that, even when you were born the most privileged person, it's no guarantee that you'll stay in that manner.

If you're among those individuals who excelled in school and then got an excellent job, you have be extra careful because you're in a position that there is no external pressure or desire to move out of. There's no reason to be struggling. You can continue to work for years without obvious negative consequences. It's not good when you are happy with the work you do and don't want to stay with the same organization for a couple of years until you are eventually promoted to a better post. Make sure to save for retirement and to make investments when opportunities arise themselves.

The majority of people live paycheck to pay day without thinking about the future. This is a dangerous place one could find yourself in. Imagine living in a city which is about to be struck by a tsunami, but you don't realize is coming until it actually hits. The effects of a tsunami could range that ranges from losing your job to a downturn in the economy (think the year 2008) to being sick and being unable to work for an extended duration of. The issue is that you had a plan for the worst case scenario, but you didn't plan for the worst. If you experience anything that isn't ideal and you aren't prepared, you will face the possibility of a difficult year after that.

I've seen individuals who started their lives in an empty cardboard box on the streets (true tale) and then ended up becoming one of the most wealthy families in America as I have witnessed wealthy families lose everything they have within a few years because of poor choices in their finances and addiction. Both are amazing and I'm certain you wouldn't have predicted the futures of these individuals if you were in their early years.

What I'm trying say by this is that no matter the place you're at in the present moment, what matters the most is what you choose to do and how happens with the time you have each and every day. The habits that make us successful are formed by the actions we make every day. You shouldn't expect to get up one day and suddenly be super productive, then sit down to create the book you've always wanted to write for a long time in four hours uninterrupted, the same way you shouldn't expect to get up one day and lift 200 pounds in the absence of ever going to the gym. If you're planning to do something big begin by setting smaller, manageable targets. If you'd like to bench 200lbs, you could begin by lifting 10 before moving to. Even if you started off in a shaky position and could not lift even 20lbs, if you keep working hard, you'll eventually reach that goal (or at the very least, the weight of 100lbs).

There are certain traits that successful people share. Being able to recognize these traits and witnessing the impact they bring to our lives is life-changing. If you're living the life of an entrepreneur it's just an issue of getting success to be able to catch up with you. This isn't about posting photos that appear on the internet of yourself with $100 bills at the front of luxury cars. I'm talking about making the work every day, without seeking praise or encouragement from outside sources. By working in silence, you will be able to keep from becoming distracted, and those who hate you aren't sure what to say.

Get up early in order to complete your tasks before the rest of the world wakes up.

Set clear and set goals, and a clear action plan that you can adhere to each day.

and try to increase value, not just to earn money and the money will follow.

CONTACTING EXTERNAL ASSURANCE

You may need to cope with pressure from your family or friends or even your partner. The resistance to change is normal and the best method to handle it is to demonstrate how much you have gained from the outcome.

Being able to manage external pressure is a lot less stressful if the pressure is from people who you only interact with only for a couple of hours a day or meet only once per week.

It is possible to tell them that you want to be able to accept your choice to live minimalist. You would like to not have negative comments about it, but should they have questions or want to discuss about your lifestyle , be willing to talk with them. Be aware that the majority of criticism stems from a lack of understanding of the situation.

Of course, it's difficult when everyone is pushing you to purchase a home or a car, get married , and have kids. It gets even more challenging in the case of living with them. If they're your siblings, parents or a partner, your decisions could affect them too particularly when you're married and are the sole owner of your finances within your home, as a poor financial decision can cause a negative effect on how you live together.

If you wish to make them aware of the reasoning behind your choice, demonstrate to them the advantages that this type of lifestyle offers. If you don't have any documentation of how it works, you can create a projection by using your current income and expenses , and another using the future earnings and expenses.

What do you think it will look like in a year? What about five or 10 years from now?

Larger numbers create a greater impact. If you tell your spouse you're saving $15,000 annually by cutting down on a few costs I'm sure they'll get enthusiastic. It's also a good idea to consider this as a motivational factor, to motivate yourself.

So, out of the amount you want to save, you could choose the percentage, for example 50% that you could spend on a trip to a place that you've been wanting to visit or to explore new dining options and experiences in the vicinity. While doing this, you'll save the remaining 50% to fund a long time goal or using a portion of it to invest in.

Some lessons on money I've learned Over the years

These are some lessons on money I've learned throughout my life through personal experience or listening to the experiences of others.

The best time to sell your item is when people are buying and in reverse, the best most appropriate time to purchase is when it's on sale. Most likely, you'll be able to sell the item at more money and aren't required to take the time needed in selling your item into account as well, whereas it's a case where everyone is selling their items however no one will be buying it, you'll be able to get the best price.

Cash is the most valuable currency. Being able to cash out is one of the most significant advantages you be an investor, particularly in times of economic downturn. One of my friend's father was able to purchase an apartment at 20% less than the cost of market because he had money in his bank account. However, I should mention that he's also an excellent negotiator as well as a real estate developer too so it wasn't like it was a matter of walking in and asked for a discount of 20. Learn to negotiate.

If everybody is doing it, there's a high probability that it's an inflated bubble. Everybody knows about it and everyone is talking about it, and everyone is learning about earning money this method (and they're earning money). These are indicators to stay clear from this possibility unless you're betting against it. Consider the Bitcoin bubble as an instance as it surpassed the $8,000 mark, people were in a frenzy of joining the trend and purchasing Bitcoin. It then reached a peak value of around $20,000 before plummeting down to $5,500 before it remained at $6,500. I'm not saying that Bitcoin is a fraud or something like that However, in this case it is clear what a bubble appears to be in the beginning, as well as after it bursts. The price could rise to $20,000 in the future , if Bitcoin is accepted as a medium of exchange, but at present the actual value of Bitcoin is about $6,500. Here is an illustration of how the value of Bitcoin has performed over the years.

It's more beneficial to own an item of a minor size than to be a that is replaceable in an entire system. This means it's much better to run your own business rather than become an employee. Why? Because , if employees are employed, they automatically can be replaced. If you're the sole owner of the company the only way to be replaced is if you choose to employ someone else to take your place. As an employee, can be a great opportunity to gain insight into how the company functions at different levels as well as get experience in the business.

It's not that I'm disliking having a job, but there are individuals who are the perfect person to fill the profile of an employee and are as valuable to an organization as the rest of us because it requires them to function effectively. Don't completely rely on a job. Begin building up savings as quickly as you can.

It's better to get 10% of the huge cake than to own 100% of the cupcake. In other words, if you are able to team with other people to increase your profits more, it's much better than being the sole owner of a small-scale business that won't generate more than. If I earn $100 per month selling my course by myself, but I can earn $1000 when I partner with someone else who is looking to market my course for a 50% commission , it's much more beneficial for us both to form the process of forming a partnership.

The money gets bored. If you're not making use of your money, and it's stored in your safe or bank account you have, it's likely to be bored. Money is always moving It wants to do its job for you and earn more money. What is the reason you are keeping it as a prisoner? It is bound to be able to escape by making illogical purchases or costly experiences.

Earning money is just half the fight. To keep it in the bank is the other part. Most people think that the hardest part of becoming wealthy is getting the money, but this is only half in the process. It is essential to know how to manage your money effectively for a chance to become wealthy.

Be kind to everyone and avoid getting involved in arguments. What does this have to do with have to do with money? All things, money (or money or wealth) is cyclical. If you are constantly picking battles with everyone you meet when you're at the topof the heap, you'll probably have to ask the chance to be

155

given the chance to prove yourself at the lowest point. It's much easier to build relationships with friends than keep enemies. It is never a good idea to think about when you'll require the help of someone else.

Consistency is the most important factor to success. If you're focused and focus on a single chance, you'll be a lot more likely to be successful than one who leaps between opportunities and never succeeds.

They are among the most important lessons I've learned over my life. If you enjoyed the publication and thought it was useful Please leave comments with your opinions about it. It's extremely beneficial and I'll always be thankful.

Now, without further delay we'll jump right to the end.

Chapter 8: Life And Goals

"Whether you think you're capable or think that you're not, you're correct"

Henry Ford Henry Ford

A while ago, I had a conversation with a man who didn't have a home since he was a traveler and that's the way his life was for the vast majority throughout his existence. He was recently back from Colombia and had traveled to Europe, the US and Spain just a couple of weeks ago. Although this isn't a common thing however, he was able to attain this level of living through the use of technology to his favor, and by creating passive income sources that took only eight hours per monthly to maintain. If you're interested in the work he's doing is that he runs a couple of small-scale software companies and sells products via Amazon FBA.

When you determine the kind of lifestyle you would like to look like You can then determine the amount of money you'll must earn per month, and what you could accomplish this. Thus, it is directly linked to your goals.

There are plenty of questions to consider about your finances and the answer is contingent on where you'd like be and what you'd like to become. If you're looking to take to retire early and you're 35, you should to get started on the process at the earliest possible time and also invest to grow your savings because saving on your own will not be enough to get there fast enough. It's no surprise that I doubt he'll ever work again at an employment unless it's with one of his numerous businesses. Once you've got an idea of the lifestyle, it's time to create a plan of action for the way you'll reach your goal.

Big goals generate action. You must create goals that are big enough to inspire you to keep going. There must be a reason to adhere with your financial plan and pursue your goals. If it's not strong enough or large enough, then you're likely to be unsuccessful since there is no benefit of spending your entire earnings for things that will bring immediate satisfaction instead of an exciting future.

Your objectives should be precise and measurable, as well as an estimated timeframe within which you will achieve your goals. It's different to earn an additional $100 at the end of the week than it is to do so in two years. If you don't set yourself an end date, you'll likely delay the steps that you have to complete to reach your goals, thinking you've got plenty of time. But you don't. So start making progress now. Your goals must be measurable as you'll need a way to gauge your progress as well as how you're from your desired goal. This will also allow you to develop a plan that will give you the daily and weekly steps you need to take to achieve your desired goal.

Your goals can be divided into particular aspects of your daily life you wish to work on.

Because this is a finance book, we'll focus on the financial part however, you can apply these strategies for setting goals for other areas , too.

These could include:

Financial/money: I earn each month _____ as passive income through

_____

Self-development:

_____

_____

Health:

_____

_____

Family:

_____

_____

Friends:

_____

_____

Spirituality:

_____

_____

I know that every person has their own objective (or objectives) in each of these areas, and there's an empty space to record your goals. Create them in a way they can inspire you. Don't be scared to imagine of the big picture.

If you believe that you are able to succeed, you'll discover a way to do that. If you think you're not capable of it, then your mind will discover ways to derail you because you're correct and we enjoy being right. In the event that we fail , we often defend ourselves with small excuses like "I knew I was not going to be able to get that increase, I'm not a good enough _____" Do not do this. You're smart and competent enough to earn the raise you want, so keep striving for it.

Question:

What are your goals this year? Sort them out by region and then write them out in an order that makes them precise, quantifiable and gives you a timeline to accomplish it. Be assured that you will meet them within that time because you'll always be working towards them. The most important thing is to get more efficient every day. It is possible to write just your financial goals, or you can include the other goals you have as well.

_____
_____
_____
_____
_____
_____
_____
_____
_____
_____
_____
_____
_____
_____
_____
_____
_____

It can be difficult to determine the things you'd like to do in the near future could be anxious but it's going aid you over the long run. My priorities changed after I realized that I wasn't thinking about the huge house and brand new car everyone else sets as their ultimate goal but instead toward liberty. Minimalism can help you achieve the level of freedom that's difficult to achieve with other means and I was not willing to compromise my freedom in exchange for an increase in income, so I needed to find a way that would meet my minimalist lifestyle as well as my goals in financial terms.

The effects of income and minimalism affect lifestyle at an incredible level The most noticeable differences were apparent in my attitude to my life, the manner in which I traveled, and the way I spent my days. I began writing down something for that I was thankful every each day, which allowed me to see that I was in a place of abundant things. I learned to travel with ease since it's all about experiences, not what you take. Finally, I learned to be mindful of my time. I stopped wasting my time every week on my social networks, and turned my attention to business books, getting more efficient and pursuing my goals instead of consuming inspirational articles.

MINDSET & HABITS

"Whatever your mind a person is able to imagine and believe in, it is possible to be achieved"

- Napoleon Hill

If I told you that there is one thing, a thing that can determine whether you'll be successful or not in any field of your life Would you trust me? You can fairly accurately predict what the life of a person will appear in six months, by studying what they're doing right now. Your future is largely contingent on your lifestyle. It's what we do every day that decides the direction we'll take in the future.

If you're overweight and you change your lifestyle to that of a healthy person, eventually you will attain the weight you need to be. If you are committed to working out 5 times a week and eating a balanced diet, it's just the matter of time until you meet the goal you have set for yourself. It is the same when you are productive and have good money habits.

The question is how long will you be able to keep going? The purpose of forming the right habit is to keep doing it. It is also important to be diligent about removing the negative habits that you've been being a part of. Certain habits can be harmful to you and are difficult to eradicate A good example is smoking cigarettes. Many people try to stop but fail since it's not an easy task and requires a level of commitment which many do not have. Therefore, they return to their old habits, which is to continue to smoke even though they are aware that this will cause harm later on. Develop habits that will improve your life so that you won't need to alter your unhealthy habits until it's too late.

The habits you develop are what make you successful. There's nothing as an instant achievement, and that overnight success was years to create. The fact that you only get to see the moment when they make it to the top does not mean that they didn't put in many hours in preparation, organizing and practicing. You don't get to see the sleepless nights they had to sleep through as they needed to complete lifting, practice programming, or editing. Youtubers, too, spend a lot of energy and time into the videos they create. They need to think up a plan of what they want to film, write a kind of draft of the topics they'll be speaking about, then film the video (sometimes multiple times as they stumble or misspell the words) and then edit the video (which involves reviewing all of the content and removing only the bits they think will be beneficial or interesting to their viewers) Find music that's available for free and then add to their videos, create the description, and come up with a captivating title that draws people to are able to click it and so on. The video of 10 minutes you've just seen took two hours to produce. Not so simple being a Youtuber now, huh? It is likely that they have to spend another two hours looking through the comments posted on the video and social media and responding to as many of them as they can since it's essential to engage with the viewers.

The first response I typically receive when I tell people that I'm a author is "Woah I'm not able to write a novel." And you are aware of what the worst part is? They're likely to be right. If you put up obstacles to what you could do, you'll never be able to accomplish it because you'd need to face every mental obstacle you put up before you begin to try. The sole reason I'm able and publish the book is because I'm dedicated to accomplishing this. Yes, it's my passion, but because it's something I like doing does not mean it's as if I stare at my computer's screen and write whatever is in my head and then put it on the internet to be published when I'm out. It requires planning and perseverance to be capable of writing a book or even complete it.

A few days ago, a man wanted to know where I got the motivation to write. I said that discipline is the first step to inspiration. Writing is when I'm motivated and also when I'm not because I've made writing every day an habit. Habits are inextricably linked with your mental outlook since this is what's going to define your future. If you're trying to improve your life, you must to alter your thinking. There's no way that you could lounge around on your couch and not doing anything and hope to make it rich over the coming year. Forget about watching television. You must change the habit to something that is more productive, like reading. In order to achieve this without falling to resistance, you require more of a motivation. Your mindset can help you avoid harmful or unproductive habits. Having an optimistic mindset will stop you from wasting your time watching television, and will force you to devote your time to activities that will be beneficial to you in the near future.

Another reason to not use the television is the time we are spending in the car. Many people utilize it to listen to music , not realizing they are studying any subject they'd like to learn about. The time we spend in traffic is a waste of time however, this doesn't mean we cannot benefit from it by listening to audiobooks about the business of sales, nutrition and architectural, economics, marketing and more. Education is a necessity to be continued after graduation to ensure that we are improving each day. I generally listen to audiobooks via Audible as well as videos from Youtube concerning a specific topic I'm looking to further my knowledge in, or whenever I need to push myself.

I've observed that one of the main reasons people end failing is that they did not consider failure something that could happen, and they believed that everything would be a success without making an effort to make a change, but ended up in the same place at the age of 60 as they were when they were in their 30s. In the event you asked any 35-year old about what they imagine their future will be at the age of 60 and 60, they'll probably claim that they're in completely different situation and living in a more comfortable area with a nicer automobile, likely nearing retirement because they're hopeful. But the reality is worse than the perception. The majority of Americans aren't able to afford retirement due to the fact that they don't have savings, or the ones they have in pension accounts is worth less than what they'll require to retire. This is a discussion of 70+ years old people who are here. Do you think this is what they'd have offered you at the age of 30?

The uncertainty and aging of the population change the way we've grown accustomed to. Fortunately, we're living in an age where you can be more prosperous by learning to make the most of the tools available to you. When you realize that you may be forced to endure two to five years to experience the life that virtually no one is able to enjoy, you're on the road to financial independence. It may be long, and certainly difficult, but it's worth it. You'll exchange 2 years of hard-work and commitment to a life of freedom. You'll be living the life no one would want to live, to live the life that no one could afford.

I'll tell you a thingabout me, I used to be a couch potato. I often talked about being a millionaire, what I wanted to become and what I wanted to become , but my actions seemed to be in the opposite direction. I would spend lots of money on things that are disposable such as food, clothes and makeup , instead of investing it into my education and myself. It was very hard for me when I realized that I was in the exact situation I was in two years ago. What could be the reason? I've been trying to become millionaire, isn't it? If you consider spending four hours a day scrolling through inspirational quotations on Instagram and watching endless Netflix shows. When I finally decided to end my old habits completely. I erased both Instagram along with Netflix on my mobile together with Candy Crush, Facebook, Pinterest and all the other apps I spent excessive time on.

With this extra time, I decided to focus on something, so I began writing books, creating blogging and , on the other hand, made Youtube videos. I was trying to figure out a way which would bring me some decent cash every month. The three models mentioned above are great sources of income, but they weren't effective for me. It wasn't like anything changed since I was putting my energy working on a variety of projects but never committing to a particular one. It wasn't a great time to earn money, but it provided me with a wealth of useful skills. I learned to design and create websites, and complete the creation process of a film from planning through filming to editing and publishing . I also learned self-motivation and discipline by writing books (not so easy as it sounds, but feasible).

One of the questions I am asking myself before I begin any business or other activity is:

Are I committed to committing two years of my life to this?

If you don't, then I don't take it up. The issue with people are that they want everything now and want to have money immediately without the effort. The issue with this can be that it is a result of value that is created, but they are conditioned to ignore this part.

It takes the average company about two years to reach a break-even. If you're not prepared to invest at least two years, you're unlikely to enjoy the rewards of expanding your business. Once you've passed breakeven and you begin realizing profits if your company is performing very well.

It is important to be sure to keep your beliefs that limit you in check as they could be a sting in the back of your neck. If you've been raised in a system that actually is punishing people who earn riches, you might have more restrictive beliefs that are hindering your progress. The belief that rich people are evil can stop you from becoming rich because you don't want be evil. Do you see where I'm getting at in this?

Why do you think money is to be bad? There's no logic to support the assertion. If someone who was wealthy suddenly turned out to be unhygienic, is because they weren't the best person to begin with. Money is a multiplier factor. If you're successful, you can achieve great things and aid millions of people. But If you're a negative person prior to acquiring the money, you'll just get worse and more sinister. It all depends on what you'd like to accomplish and how you would like to stand out.

Another method in which money can be a multiplier is when you plan to establish a company, it's not an option to begin with what's in your account. You'll need to start with a large budget you can put in R&D and IT, marketing as well as sales department.

Who also told you that the money was scarce? Maybe you've not found an opportunity to get it as of yet. If you've traded on the stock market, you could make $1100 in about three minutes. Of course, you'll need to train for this , but it's achievable. The market capitalization of

Apple is around \$1 trillion. If that's not evidence enough to show that there's actually money to be found I don't even know what else is. The problem is that somebody else is holding it and it's your money. You are entitled to be rich and enjoy your life without stressing about money every month.

It's a lot more enjoyable living in abundance, and you will make a lot of good doing it.

If you're left with nothing to lose, then why are you wasting time? If you're starting from low, then there's only one direction to go, and that is upwards.

Question:

What are some of the beliefs that limit you that you are holding? They can be related to your finances or yourself. You must identify them so that you can begin working to correct them.

_____

_____

_____

_____

_____

_____

_____

_____

_____

_____

_____

_____

_____

_____

_____

_____

_____

I'm sure one of the most difficult things when you begin your journey towards financial freedom is believing in your abilities. I was fortunate enough to have positive people, and I had one mentor who always motivated me with his faith in my ability succeed. You could be more fortunate and have more people who support you or perhaps not as lucky and be surrounded with loved people who are unable to motivate you.

Whatever the situation I'd like to assure you that I believe in you.

I am convinced that you can succeed in everything you desire and more. You've got everything you need to succeed and meet every goal you set to bring your dreams to life.

Even if you aren't sure in yourself I'm convinced that you are. If you've been looking for an opportunity to start the journey toward the life you goals, this is the time.

You have complete charge in your personal life.

WHAT CAN YOU DO TO INCREASE YOUR NET COMMUNITY

We've already discussed this earlier in the chapter, but I wanted to focus on it because I believe that having more money can enable you to live a better life. If you're looking to invest your money in holidays, a better house, or invest in education, money allows you the opportunity to spend it however you want without having to think about how you'll manage it.

Value

The first step is to identify something that people want and will spend money on. It can be anything in high demand, and without any or low competitors as it's simpler to position your business in this way. If you are entering an industry that is highly competitive consumers will have no reason to purchase your product unless it's distinctive in a manner that is appealing to the buyers. There is no need to come up with anything completely new, you just need to look for one element of a the product that you could be improved.

Reach

How many people do you have the ability to connect with your business or position you're working in currently?

Let's use KDP to illustrate. when I create a book through Amazon then it can reach anyone who uses Amazon or has English and is looking for the book that covers this topic.

It's the same for blogs or social media account. You are essentially able to reach the entire world without the hassle of having to grow like physical outlets like Subway and Subway, which you can still find in almost every part of the world. It is essential to discover a way to market your product to a wider audience and only achieve this by contacting larger audiences. This can be done by using the internet, and even sell your product online using the assistance of a distributor or Amazon FBA.

Market Research

It's not enjoyable to think of an idea, create it, execute the entire selling and marketing strategy and then invest in R&D manufacturing the product, and then not even sell one product when you launch.

This is something that be prevented at all cost.

A quick failure is the best option for you since it's much less expensive to correct an error in the beginning stages than to correct it on before the day of the launch. This not only saves your money, however, but will also save time and resources and costs.

Marketing

It doesn't matter if have the greatest product ever developed but if nobody ever hears about it, and your business goes under in the space of a few months because you didn't attract customers.

One of my most favorite quotes I've heard over the last year is from one of the founding members of Airbnb in which he stated that they would keep innovating because if you launch and nobody notices, you will be able to launch over and over until something occurs. A launch is a fantastic method to increase the amount of people who are likely to use your service or platform.

It is also important to keep in mind that certain things require time, and it's likely that you will not begin with a large revenue immediately. Coca-Cola began selling just 9 servings a day in its very first year. Are you able to guess the amount they are selling today?

In the realm of marketing, it is essential to think outside the box in order to come up with the best way to make your clients think about you often.

There's also an enormous advantage when advertising during a sale time like Black Friday or Cyber Monday and also during Amazon Prime day. If you're not aware of this happening as an entrepreneur, you'll see a spike in your sales due to the huge amount of traffic to Amazon on those days. Imagine if you'd thought of the impact and put processes in place to ride the trend. Consider yourself more of a producer than being a consumer, and you'll find endless ways to earn money.

I'm always amazed by the way brands such as Apple almost always make a product available and make money from it (guilty as it is). After you've seen the new iPhone, there's something in you that says it's essential and you find ways to buy it. This is often the reason why you go into debt in order to get the latest phone and is not a wise financial decision. What I'm trying to show by this is that you must strive to attract loyal customers like Apple's.

Growth

My dad always reminds me to keep in mind that even elephants begin small. I remember feeling very angry in the past due to the fact that I was running a business that did not produce as much as I expected it to. I felt like I was at it for hours every each day. A few days later, I realized the company itself was growing at an incredible rate for any business nearly 150% per month, but I had not realized this because the first growth was so insignificant that it wasn't even evident. It wasn't until the 2nd year that it increased to the point that it became viable and began to generate more than I ever thought possible. If you look at it in relation to the elephant's saying that it's a good thing, it is logical.

Pregnancies for elephants last almost two years, two years during which it is impossible to be able to see the baby elephant, however, it's there and growing, getting bigger and larger every month. It begins with a tiny baby that is so small that it's unnoticeable. Even when elephants are born , they're tiny in comparison to adult elephants that could weigh up to 6,300 kilograms. When you consider that they're born at a weight of about 100 kg and are already larger than most human beings, however they're 1.5 percent larger than one of the male adult elephants. The thing is, even if you don't see the results you want right now, but working hard regularly, eventually you'll arrive at. The fact that you're starting from scratch doesn't mean that you're not capable of growing to a massive size and eventually become a powerful and strong elephant.

Find a way to create an additional or even third income stream. The most reliable income you could get is passive income as it doesn't rely on your availability to earn money. You earn money as you're asleep and because it is a global business, it is a huge market and even those in China, India, Europe or Hawaii might be reading the blog you published earlier in the day, and earn you money in Ad revenues or affiliates.

Scalability and Replicability

If you create an organization that is easily duplicated, you have a model that is able to and probably be replicated by others, in different cities or in other countries and also for different businesses, so long as the needed adjustments are implemented.